the Tofu for Health cookbook

the Tofu for Health cookbook

recipes with style and taste

Wendy Sweetser

TIME LIFE BOOKS

Alexandria, Virginia

TIME LIFE BOOKS

Time-Life Books is a division of Time Life Inc.
Time-Life is a trademark of Time Warner Inc. and affiliated companies.

TIME LIFE INC.
Chairman and Chief Executive Officer: Jim Nelson
President and Chief Operating Officer: Steven Janas
Senior Executive Vice President and Chief Operations Officer: Mary Davis Holt
Senior Vice President and Chief Financial Officer: Christopher Hearing

TIME-LIFE BOOKS
President: Larry Jellen
Senior Vice President, New Markets: Bridget Boel
Vice President, Home and Hearth Markets: Nicholas M. DiMarco
Vice President, Content Development: Jennifer L. Pearce

TIME-LIFE TRADE PUBLISHING
Vice President and Publisher: Neil S. Levin
Senior Sales Director: Richard J. Vreeland
Director, Marketing and Publicity: Inger Forland
Director of Trade Sales: Dana Hobson
Director of Custom Publishing: John Lalor
Director of Rights and Licensing: Olga Vezeris

THE TOFU FOR HEALTH COOKBOOK
Director of New Product Development: Carolyn M. Clark
New Product Development Manager: Lori A. Woehrle
Senior Editor: Linda Bellamy
Director of Design: Kate L. McConnell
Project Editor: Jennie Halfant

This book was designed and produced by
Quintet Publishing Limited
6 Blundell Street
London N7 7BH

Senior Project Editor: Laura Price
Editor: Margaret Gilbey
Nutritionist: Fiona Hunter
Art Directors: Labeena Ishaque, Sharanjit Dhol
Designer: Axis Design
Photographer: Ian Garlick
Home Economist: Kathryn Hawkins

Creative Director: Richard Dewing

Typeset in Great Britain by Central Southern Typesetters, Eastbourne
Manufactured in Hong Kong by Regent Publishing Services Ltd.
Printed in China by Leefung-Asco Printers Ltd.

© 2001 Quintet Publishing.

10 9 8 7 6 5 4 3 2 1

School and library distribution by Time-Life Education, P.O. Box 85026, Richmond,
Virginia 23285-5026.

Library of Congress Cataloging-in-Publication Data available upon request:
Librarian, Time-Life Books
2000 Duke Street
Alexandria, Virginia 22314

ISBN 0-7370-1625-6

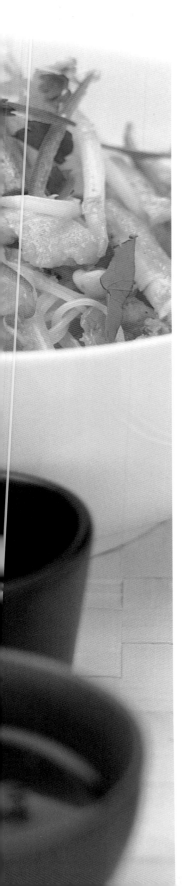

Contents

INTRODUCTION

The Chinese people first identified soy bean curd, popularly known as tofu, as a wonderfood some 2,000 years ago. Chinese scholars credit the development of tofu to a Taoist prince of the Han dynasty in the second century BC, but a millennium passed before it found its way to Japan via Manchuria and Korea—where tofu shops are now to be found everywhere. Today, tofu remains a staple food for billions of Southeast Asian people who exploit its versatility in rice, noodle, stir-fry, and steamed dishes. For many of them, soybeans, in the form of tofu and other related products, are their meat, milk, cheese, bread, and oil and, in fact, tofu is actually known as "cheese."

WHY TOFU?

On the healthy eating scale, tofu scores full marks every time. Why then, when so many of us are attempting to cut back on our fat and carbohydrate intake or just trying to eat more healthily, are so few of us willing to give tofu a try? Food writers up till now have tended to extol the virtues of tofu as the cornerstone of a vegan or vegetarian diet but have neglected to demonstrate how valuable it can be when included in ordinary, everyday recipes as part of a "normal" diet. Unlike many other Asian foods, tofu has yet to establish itself as a popular ingredient in Western cooking; despite all the food scares and ever-growing obsession with eating healthily, the majority of people will still tell you they don't like tofu whether they have actually tried it or not. If a product ever needed a spin doctor to improve its image, it is tofu.

Next time you are making a pie, a burger, or Bolognese sauce, if you replace half the meat with tofu you have immediately lowered the animal fat content by 50 percent but forfeited virtually none of the texture or flavor. Half cream and half tofu used in place of all cream in a chocolate dessert, mousse, or brulée will make the calorie count tumble and by mixing tofu with other ingredients in a stir-fry, salad, quiche, or even a curry you will discover an easy and satisfying way to improve your diet without spoiling the pleasure you derive from eating good food.

Showing how you can incorporate tofu into an ordinary, everyday diet is what this cookbook sets out to do. It is not aimed solely at the crash-dieter, the weight-watcher, the vegan, or the food faddist, although all will hopefully find something in it for them. It is for anyone who likes to eat well but who wants to watch their diet a little more, anyone seeking

BELOW Assorted types of tofu prepared for cooking

to cut back on their meat and dairy intake but not wanting to avoid those products altogether, or anyone, whatever their age and lifestyle, seeking a varied, balanced, healthier way of eating without resorting to a drastic change of diet. If any of those people sound like you, then give tofu a try—you could be surprised at how much you like it!

ABOVE Regular tofu

HOW IS IT MADE?

Tofu is made from soy milk, using a process similar to cheesemaking. It takes around one hour to turn soybeans into a block of tofu.

The beans are first washed and rinsed to remove impurities and then ground into a paste. They are then cooked to extract the protein from them to make the soy milk. At this stage a moist, crumbly, white fiber called okara is extracted as a by-product from the milk. This high-protein, low-calorie food can be bought separately in Asian food stores and it is used for making vegetarian pâtés or burgers, or added to mixes for pancakes, cookies, tart shells, and crisp batter coatings.

After the okara has been extracted, the soy milk is boiled and a coagulant then added to turn the milk into curds, which are pressed. The whey is drained off and the resulting block of tofu is cut and packaged and ready for sale.

ARE THERE DIFFERENT TYPES OF TOFU?

Standard tofu comes in various degrees of firmness and is graded according to how much water a block contains. You will probably find three different styles of standard tofu—extra firm, firm, and soft—on sale in Asian food stores and health shops, but supermarkets are likely only to offer one choice of packet simply marked "tofu." Another style, "silken" is available from Asian stores. To avoid confusion, the following may be a useful guide:

EXTRA FIRM OR REGULAR TOFU

This has been pressed for the longest time so it has the lowest water content and is firm enough to slice and dice. Available from speciality stores, you are unlikely to find it on sale in supermarkets. However, a block of supermarket tofu frozen in its package and then defrosted will firm up sufficiently to be grated.

FIRM TOFU

An all-purpose tofu and the one usually sold in supermarkets; therefore the most widely available and the most versatile. Firm enough to be cut into cubes or slices, it can also be used in recipes requiring soft tofu, as long as sufficient extra water is added to achieve the necessary consistency.

SOFT TOFU

Pressed for the shortest time, so it has more of the whey left in. Soft and smooth, it is usually puréed to make soups, sauces, creamy desserts, or dressings as it is not firm enough to dice or slice. As mentioned above, if soft tofu is needed for a recipe and not available, firm tofu can be substituted as long as extra water is added.

ABOVE Soft tofu

SILKEN TOFU

This Japanese product is made slightly differently from standard tofu as it is poured into pots and left to set instead of being pressed. The curds and whey are not separated, so the resulting tofu is creamy, smooth, and similar in style to full-fat Greek yogurt. Use for dressings, drinks, desserts, and sauces.

LEFT Silken tofu

More unusual types of tofu available

SMOKED TOFU

Firm and spongy in texture with a rich, brown crust, this is smoked regular tofu with an attractive "char-grilled" flavor. It can be eaten without being cooked in salads, sandwiches, and stuffings, cut into sticks to serve with dips, or grilled, fried, or sautéed.

MARINATED TOFU

Many recipes suggest marinating tofu in flavorings such as soy sauce and ginger before cooking, and some premarinated tofu products are available from supermarkets. Use in stir-fry dishes, braises, or Asian-style salads.

ABOVE Smoked tofu

DEEP-FRIED TOFU

Known as "tauhu goreng," this Chinese product from Singapore is available from Asian stores. Serve with a soy sauce or chili dip as an appetizer or add to noodle and rice dishes.

DO-IT-YOURSELF TOFU

Packets of long-life, powdered tofu are available from some Chinese supermarkets to make up yourself. However, most ready-to-use supermarket tofu is vacuum packed with a long shelf life, so storing tofu is not a problem.

ABOVE Deep-fried tofu

RIGHT Firm tofu

to cut back on their meat and dairy intake but not wanting to avoid those products altogether, or anyone, whatever their age and lifestyle, seeking a varied, balanced, healthier way of eating without resorting to a drastic change of diet. If any of those people sound like you, then give tofu a try—you could be surprised at how much you like it!

ABOVE Regular tofu

HOW IS IT MADE?

Tofu is made from soy milk, using a process similar to cheesemaking. It takes around one hour to turn soybeans into a block of tofu.

The beans are first washed and rinsed to remove impurities and then ground into a paste. They are then cooked to extract the protein from them to make the soy milk. At this stage a moist, crumbly, white fiber called okara is extracted as a by-product from the milk. This high-protein, low-calorie food can be bought separately in Asian food stores and it is used for making vegetarian pâtés or burgers, or added to mixes for pancakes, cookies, tart shells, and crisp batter coatings.

After the okara has been extracted, the soy milk is boiled and a coagulant then added to turn the milk into curds, which are pressed. The whey is drained off and the resulting block of tofu is cut and packaged and ready for sale.

ARE THERE DIFFERENT TYPES OF TOFU?

Standard tofu comes in various degrees of firmness and is graded according to how much water a block contains. You will probably find three different styles of standard tofu—extra firm, firm, and soft—on sale in Asian food stores and health shops, but supermarkets are likely only to offer one choice of packet simply marked "tofu." Another style, "silken" is available from Asian stores. To avoid confusion, the following may be a useful guide:

EXTRA FIRM OR REGULAR TOFU

This has been pressed for the longest time so it has the lowest water content and is firm enough to slice and dice. Available from speciality stores, you are unlikely to find it on sale in supermarkets. However, a block of supermarket tofu frozen in its package and then defrosted will firm up sufficiently to be grated.

FIRM TOFU

An all-purpose tofu and the one usually sold in supermarkets; therefore the most widely available and the most versatile. Firm enough to be cut into cubes or slices, it can also be used in recipes requiring soft tofu, as long as sufficient extra water is added to achieve the necessary consistency.

SOFT TOFU

Pressed for the shortest time, so it has more of the whey left in. Soft and smooth, it is usually puréed to make soups, sauces, creamy desserts, or dressings as it is not firm enough to dice or slice. As mentioned above, if soft tofu is needed for a recipe and not available, firm tofu can be substituted as long as extra water is added.

ABOVE Soft tofu

SILKEN TOFU

This Japanese product is made slightly differently from standard tofu as it is poured into pots and left to set instead of being pressed. The curds and whey are not separated, so the resulting tofu is creamy, smooth, and similar in style to full-fat Greek yogurt. Use for dressings, drinks, desserts, and sauces.

LEFT Silken tofu

More unusual types of tofu available

ABOVE Smoked tofu

SMOKED TOFU

Firm and spongy in texture with a rich, brown crust, this is smoked regular tofu with an attractive "char-grilled" flavor. It can be eaten without being cooked in salads, sandwiches, and stuffings, cut into sticks to serve with dips, or grilled, fried, or sautéed.

MARINATED TOFU

Many recipes suggest marinating tofu in flavorings such as soy sauce and ginger before cooking, and some premarinated tofu products are available from supermarkets. Use in stir-fry dishes, braises, or Asian-style salads.

ABOVE Deep-fried tofu

DEEP-FRIED TOFU

Known as "tauhu goreng," this Chinese product from Singapore is available from Asian stores. Serve with a soy sauce or chili dip as an appetizer or add to noodle and rice dishes.

DO-IT-YOURSELF TOFU

Packets of long-life, powdered tofu are available from some Chinese supermarkets to make up yourself. However, most ready-to-use supermarket tofu is vacuum packed with a long shelf life, so storing tofu is not a problem.

Nutrition and health

The health benefits of tofu are so many and varied that they could fill a section of this book on their own. Not only is it rich in vegetable protein, but it contains all eight essential amino acids, is low in saturated fats and carbohydrates and is cholesterol-free. And, as its protein is vegetable rather than animal derived, tofu is free of the high levels of chemical toxins that can occur in meat-, dairy-, or fish-derived protein foods. It is also an excellent source of calcium for anyone with an allergy to milk, cheese, or other dairy products and is made in a simple, natural way. All in all, if you were seeking to identify the perfect food, tofu comes pretty close to the culinary ideal.

As well as being a natural and wholesome food, tofu is very low in saturated fats (1 gram per 100 grams), low in carbohydrates (1.7 grams per 100 grams of which 0.7 gram is sugar), and high in vegetable protein (11 grams per 100 grams).

It contains 4 grams of dietary fiber per 100 grams, is cholesterol-free and rich in calcium, linoleic acid, and lecithin, soybeans being the only legume that is a complete protein containing all eight essential amino acids that our bodies cannot manufacture for themselves. In addition, tofu contains vitamins B and E, choline, iron, potassium, and phosphorus.

Linoleic acid and lecithin both help to clear the arteries and vital organs of existing deposits of cholesterol in our blood, so tofu can play a useful part in helping keep heart disease and high blood pressure at bay.

Tofu is also valuable for people of all ages with special dietary needs such as those who need extra calcium. Growing children, nursing mothers, women going through the menopause, and the elderly need to ensure a good intake of calcium to keep bones and teeth healthy, but for those with allergies to dairy products or who simply dislike milk and cheese, getting enough calcium can present problems. Once again, tofu provides the answer.

ABOVE Tofu can be added to most dishes, even soups, without diminishing the taste or look of the dish. See Watercress, orange, and tofu soup on page 14.

In Southeast Asia, where tofu and other soy products are an important part of everyday diets, people are less prone to heart disease, prostate, breast, and ovarian cancers, osteoporosis, and menopausal symptoms. It is a fact that Japanese men are five times less likely to have a heart attack than those in the West and while exercise, smoking, and other lifestyle factors obviously play their part, diet must also form part of the equation.

1 soups and salads

Tofu makes a great addition to soups and salads. Low in fat and high in protein, tofu provides an extra dimension to these dishes. In soups, puréed tofu gives a creamy texture, or can be added in cubes to create firm mouthfuls infused with the flavors of the soup. Dressed salads also impart their flavor to the tofu and it can be used as a substitute for traditional ingredients—such as full-fat cheeses—or as a meat substitute to reduce cholesterol in a dish or to provide a vegetarian option.

LEFT thai beef and tofu salad (page 32)

watercress, orange, and tofu soup

SERVES 4

2 ¾ cups chicken or vegetable broth

1 ¼ cups potatoes, peeled and cut into small chunks

1 bunch watercress, coarse stalks removed

⅝ cup fresh orange juice

9 oz soft tofu

2 Tbsp butter

2 leeks, sliced thin

1 zucchini, grated

Salt and pepper

Blanched shredded leek and snipped chives, to garnish

Crusty bread, to serve

A HEARTY VEGETABLE SOUP THICKENED WITH PURÉED TOFU. IF FIRM TOFU IS MORE READILY AVAILABLE, IT CAN BE USED INSTEAD OF SOFT, BUT EXTRA BROTH OR WATER MAY BE NEEDED TO ACHIEVE THE RIGHT CONSISTENCY.

1 In a large saucepan, bring the broth to a boil. Add the potatoes, cover the pan, and simmer for 10 minutes or until tender. Chop the watercress and add to the pan. Simmer for 5 minutes.

2 Pour the soup into a food processor, add the orange juice and tofu, and purée until smooth.

3 Rinse out the saucepan and place over a low heat. Add the butter and, when foaming, sauté the leeks and zucchini until soft. Pour in the puréed soup and season to taste.

4 Reheat gently without boiling, garnish with blanched shredded leek and snipped chives, and serve with crusty bread.

nutrition facts	
energy	170 cal
	707 kJ
protein	5 g
fat	9 g
of which saturated	4 g
carbohydrate	14 g
fiber	2.5 g
cholesterol	14 mg
sodium	235 mg

pumpkin and tofu soup

SERVES 6

1 large onion, peeled and chopped

1 large potato, peeled and cut into small chunks

3½ cups prepared pumpkin flesh, cut into small chunks

1 large carrot, sliced

3¾ cups vegetable broth

1½ cups fresh orange juice

1 Tbsp brown sugar

9 oz firm tofu

Salt and pepper

6 Tbsp yogurt, plain, black pepper, and snipped fresh chives, to garnish

YOU WILL NEED A 2½-POUND PUMPKIN TO MAKE THE SOUP. CUT IT INTO HALVES, CUT AWAY THE RIND AND STALK, AND PULL OUT THE SEEDS AND FIBERS FROM THE CENTER. THE SEEDS CAN BE CRACKED OPEN AND THE KERNELS USED AS A GARNISH FOR THE SOUP.

1 Put the onion, potato, pumpkin, carrot, broth, orange juice, and sugar in a saucepan and bring to a boil. Cover the pan, lower the heat, and simmer for 40 minutes or until the vegetables are very tender.

2 Allow to cool for 30 minutes, then liquidize in batches with the tofu in a food processor or blender. Return to the pan and add enough cold water to bring to the desired consistency.

3 Reheat the soup when ready to serve, and season to taste. Spoon into bowls and garnish each serving with a spoonful of yogurt, black pepper, and chives.

nutrition facts	
energy	150 cal
	620 kJ
protein	8 g
fat	3 g
of which saturated	0.5 g
carbohydrate	24 g
fiber	3 g
cholesterol	2 mg
sodium	270 mg

tofu minestrone

SERVES 6

2 Tbsp olive oil

2 medium carrots, peeled and finely diced

1 medium onion, peeled and finely chopped

1 medium turnip, peeled and finely diced

2¾ cups vegetable broth

2¾ cups tomato pasta sauce

2 tsp pesto

9 oz firm tofu, cut into small cubes

2 ribs celery, thinly sliced

1 large zucchini, sliced

¾ cup French beans, trimmed and cut into short lengths

14-oz can cannellini beans, drained and rinsed

2 tsp chopped fresh sage

Grated Parmesan cheese, to garnish

MAKE THE SOUP SEVERAL HOURS AHEAD OR EVEN THE DAY BEFORE NEEDED SO THAT THE TOFU HAS TIME TO ABSORB THE TOMATO AND HERB FLAVORS. THE TRADITIONAL GARNISH FOR MINESTRONE IS GRATED PARMESAN—BUY A BLOCK OF CHEESE RATHER THAN READY-GRATED AS IT WILL HAVE A FRESHER FLAVOR.

1 Heat the oil in a large pan, add the carrots, onion, and turnip, and sauté for 5 minutes.

2 Pour in the broth and tomato pasta sauce, and add the pesto and tofu. Bring to a boil, lower the heat, cover, and simmer gently for 25 minutes.

3 Add the celery, zucchini, French beans, cannellini beans, and sage, and simmer for 15 minutes more or until all the vegetables are tender.

4 Ladle into deep soup bowls and garnish each serving with grated Parmesan.

nutrition facts	
energy	210 cal
	875 kJ
protein	11 g
fat	8 g
of which saturated	1 g
carbohydrate	23 g
fiber	5.5 g
cholesterol	0 mg
sodium	772 mg

chili **chicken** and tofu broth

SERVES 4

2 Tbsp peanut or vegetable oil

2 garlic cloves, peeled and finely chopped

1 Tbsp Thai red curry paste

1 cup coconut cream

2 boneless chicken breasts, cut into bite-size pieces

9 oz firm tofu, cut into bite-size pieces

3¾ cups chicken broth

2 Tbsp fish sauce

Juice of 1 lime

1 tsp brown sugar

2 cups medium dried egg noodles

Finely chopped scallion and finely sliced red chile, to garnish

MAKE THE SOUP AHEAD SO THE TOFU AND CHICKEN HAVE TIME TO ABSORB THE FLAVOR OF THE SPICES. COOK THE NOODLES JUST BEFORE SERVING AND SPOON THE REHEATED SOUP OVER THEM IN DEEP BOWLS.

1 In a large saucepan or wok, heat the oil and sauté the garlic until golden. Add the curry paste and cook for 30 seconds.

2 Stir in the coconut cream and cook for 1 minute, then add the chicken pieces, tofu, broth, fish sauce, lime juice, and brown sugar. Bring to simmering point and simmer over a low heat for 10 minutes. Remove from the heat and set aside for 1 to 2 hours or until ready to serve.

3 Cook the noodles in a pan of boiling water according to package instructions. Reheat the soup until simmering.

4 Drain the noodles and divide among four serving bowls. Spoon over the soup and serve garnished with chopped scallion and fine slices of red chile.

nutrition facts	
energy	540 cal
	2252 kJ
protein	29 g
fat	26 g
of which saturated	13 g
carbohydrate	43 g
fiber	1.5 g
cholesterol	49 mg
sodium	707 mg

roasted **tomato**, red bell **pepper**, and tofu soup

SERVES 6

6 red bell peppers, quartered and seeded

8 large ripe tomatoes, cut into halves

9 oz firm tofu, cubed

3 Tbsp olive oil

1 tsp sugar

2 tsp chopped fresh marjoram

Salt and pepper

1 red onion, peeled and finely chopped

2 garlic cloves, peeled and crushed

3½ cups vegetable broth

Shredded basil leaves, to garnish

THE BEST WAY TO PURÉE A TOMATO IS TO PUSH IT THROUGH A FOOD MILL SO THAT ANY BITTER SEEDS OR SKINS ARE CAUGHT IN ITS SIEVE AND JUST THE FLESH GOES INTO THE SOUP.

1 Preheat the oven to 375°F. Spread out the peppers, skin side up, tomatoes, and tofu cubes in a shallow roasting pan. Drizzle over 2 tablespoons of the olive oil and sprinkle with the sugar and marjoram. Season and roast in the oven for 45 minutes.

2 Heat the remaining olive oil in a large pan, add the onion and garlic, cover, and cook gently until soft but not browned. Add the roasted vegetables and tofu, then the broth, and bring to a boil.

3 Remove from the heat and cool a little before puréeing. Adjust the seasoning and add extra water or broth to bring to the desired consistency if necessary. Reheat when ready to serve and garnish each bowl with shredded basil leaves.

nutrition facts	
energy	135 cal
	566 kJ
protein	7 g
fat	4 g
of which saturated	0.5 g
carbohydrate	20 g
fiber	5 g
cholesterol	0 mg
sodium	266 mg

miso soup with shredded chicken

SERVES 4

1 cup Japanese noodles (udon or ramen)

2 tsp vegetable oil

3½ cups dashi or vegetable broth

2 Tbsp red miso paste

3 Tbsp mirin (sweet rice wine)

2½ cups shiitake mushrooms, cut into quarters

1 bunch of enoki mushrooms, separated

8 scallions, trimmed and chopped

5 oz tofu, cut into ½-in cubes

1 chicken breast, cut into ½-in pieces

4 large spinach leaves, coarse stalks removed

MISO IS A FERMENTED PASTE OF SOYBEANS, RICE, OR BARLEY THAT, WHEN MIXED WITH DASHI— A BROTH OF KONBU SEAWEED AND DRIED BONITO (FISH)—MAKES A VERY POPULAR SOUP IN JAPAN. PACKAGES OF INSTANT DASHI BROTH ARE AVAILABLE FROM LARGER SUPERMARKETS AND ASIAN STORES, AND JUST NEED RECONSTITUTING WITH BOILING WATER.

1 Cook the noodles according to package instructions. Drain, rinse under cold water, and toss with the oil to prevent them from sticking together. Set aside.

2 Pour the dashi or broth into a large pan and bring to a boil. In a small bowl, mix 4 tablespoons of the hot broth with the miso paste until blended, then gradually stir back into the pan. Add the mirin and simmer for 5 minutes. Add the mushrooms, scallions, tofu, and chicken, and simmer for 5 more minutes.

3 Shred the spinach leaves finely and stir in with the noodles. Cook for a couple of minutes until the spinach wilts and the noodles have heated through.

4 Ladle into deep soup bowls and serve at once.

nutrition facts	
energy	290 cal
	1213 kJ
protein	19 g
fat	7 g
of which saturated	1 g
carbohydrate	34 g
fiber	2.5 g
cholesterol	16 mg
sodium	502 mg

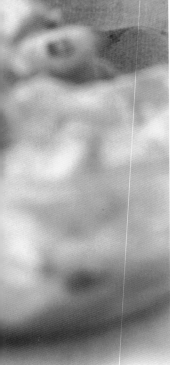

gado gado

SERVES 4

FOR THE PEANUT DRESSING:

1 tsp fresh lemon grass purée

1 garlic clove, peeled and crushed

1 tsp chili sauce

2 Tbsp sunflower oil

½ cup crunchy peanut butter

¾ cup coconut milk

Juice of 1 lime

2 tsp brown sugar

2 tsp dark sweet soy sauce

9 oz firm tofu, cut into small cubes

FOR THE SALAD:

1 cup sweet potato, diced

2 medium carrots, peeled and sliced thin

½ cup green beans, cut into ½-in lengths

½ cucumber, sliced

2 pineapple rings, cut into small pieces

½ cup bean sprouts

½ cup bok choy, shredded

Chopped red chile, to garnish

THIS IS A TRADITIONAL INDONESIAN SALAD COMBINING RAW AND COOKED VEGETABLES. HERE, CUBES OF TOFU ARE PART OF THE PEANUT AND COCONUT DRESSING.

1 For the dressing, place all the ingredients except the tofu in a bowl and beat together until smooth. Stir in the tofu and set aside for at least 1 hour.

2 To make the salad, cook the sweet potato and carrots in a pan of boiling water for 5 minutes or until tender. Drain and refresh in cold water. Pat dry with paper towels.

3 Blanch the beans in a pan of boiling water for 1 minute, drain, refresh, and pat dry. Mix the cooked vegetables with the cucumber, pineapple pieces, bean sprouts, and shredded bok choy. Pile the vegetable mixture in a serving dish. Spoon over the peanut and tofu dressing, garnish with the chopped red chile, and serve at once.

nutrition facts	
energy	450 cal
	1877 kJ
protein	14 g
fat	30 g
of which saturated	10 g
carbohydrate	30 g
fiber	6 g
cholesterol	0 mg
sodium	307 mg

greek **salad** and smoked tofu **wraps**

SERVES 4

7 oz smoked tofu, cubed

2 Tbsp olive oil

1 zucchini, sliced

4 flat breads

4 Tbsp hummus

2 large tomatoes, cut into wedges

12 pitted black olives

1 shallot, peeled and thinly sliced

1 cup feta cheese, cubed

¾ cup arugula leaves

USE FLAT BREADS TO MAKE THE WRAPS OR SLIT OPEN PITA BREAD AND PILE THE FILLING INTO THE POCKET.

1 Toss the tofu cubes with the olive oil and sear on a very hot griddle or heavy skillet for 2 minutes, turning over once or twice. Remove and add the zucchini slices to the pan. Cook for 5 minutes until the slices are softened and scorched on both sides.

2 Spread the flat breads with the hummus and divide the tofu, zucchini slices, tomato wedges, olives, sliced shallot, feta, and arugula leaves among them. Roll up and serve.

nutrition facts	
energy	500 cal
	2129 kJ
protein	22 g
fat	20 g
of which saturated	7 g
carbohydrate	64 g
fiber	4 g
cholesterol	26 mg
sodium	1450 mg

caesar salad with smoked tofu

SERVES 4

2 large, thick slices of day-old white bread

2 Tbsp olive oil

1 tsp paprika

2 very small lettuces, leaves separated

¼ cup arugula leaves

7 oz smoked tofu, cut into julienne pieces

8 anchovy fillets

½ cup Parmesan shavings

FOR THE DRESSING:

2 garlic cloves, peeled and crushed

1 Tbsp balsamic vinegar

1 Tbsp white wine vinegar

1 Tbsp Dijon mustard

Salt and pepper

6 Tbsp olive oil

1 egg

TRADITIONAL CAESAR SALAD DRESSING IS MADE WITH LIGHTLY COOKED EGG, SO IF YOU PREFER TO AVOID EATING EGGS THAT HAVE NOT BEEN FULLY COOKED, BUY A BOTTLE OF READY-MADE CAESAR DRESSING INSTEAD.

1 Cut the bread into ½-in cubes. Toss with the olive oil and paprika, and spread out on a baking sheet. Preheat the oven to 425°F and bake the bread cubes for 6 to 8 minutes until crisp and golden.

2 Mix the lettuce and arugula leaves together in a bowl and add the tofu and anchovy fillets, snipped into fine pieces. Scatter the Parmesan shavings and bread croutons on top.

3 For the dressing, mix together the crushed garlic, vinegars, mustard, and seasoning in a bowl. Gradually whisk in the oil in a thin stream until thickened. Boil the egg for 2 minutes only, cool under cold water, then remove the shell and whisk into the dressing until evenly mixed in. Pour the dressing over the salad, toss well, and serve at once.

nutrition facts	
energy	380 cal
	1564 kJ
protein	14 g
fat	32 g
of which saturated	4.5 g
carbohydrate	10g
fiber	45g
cholesterol	71 mg
sodium	500 mg

fruity **ham** and tofu salad

SERVES 4

9 oz firm tofu, cubed

¾ cup extra-virgin olive oil

4 Tbsp white wine vinegar

1 tsp Dijon mustard

1 Tbsp chopped fresh marjoram

2 Tbsp snipped chives

Salt and pepper

¾ cup frisée lettuce

4 slices of ham

2 ribs of celery, sliced

8 fresh apricots, pitted, and sliced, or 12 dried apricots, chopped

1 red-skinned apple, quartered, cored, and thinly sliced

¾ cup green seedless grapes

French bread, to serve

USE FRESH APRICOTS FOR THE SALAD WHEN THEY ARE IN SEASON, OTHERWISE, SUBSTITUTE READY-TO-EAT DRIED APRICOTS.

1 Place the tofu cubes in a shallow dish. Whisk together the olive oil, vinegar, and mustard until smooth. Stir in the marjoram and chives, and season to taste. Pour over the tofu to coat, cover the dish, and leave in a cool place for 2 hours.

2 Wash and dry the frisée lettuce and place in a large serving bowl. Cut the ham into strips and place on top with the celery, apricots, apple slices, and grapes. Spoon on the tofu, drizzling over any dressing remaining in the dish.

3 Serve at once with French bread.

nutrition facts	
energy	390 cal
	1616 kJ
protein	11 g
fat	31 g
of which saturated	4 g
carbohydrate	17 g
fiber	3 g
cholesterol	0 mg
sodium	66 mg

tofu **panzanella**

SERVES 4

8 thick slices from a ciabatta loaf

6 Tbsp extra-virgin olive oil

Fine sea salt and freshly ground black pepper

8 cherry tomatoes, cut into halves or quarters

1 small cucumber, diced

1 red onion, peeled and finely chopped

1 rib of celery, sliced

1 carrot, peeled and finely diced

9 oz firm tofu, cut into small cubes

4 Tbsp rice vinegar

2 Tbsp small basil leaves

MAKE THE SALAD A COUPLE OF HOURS BEFORE REQUIRED SO THAT THE TOFU HAS TIME TO FULLY ABSORB THE FLAVORS OF THE DRESSING AND THE HERBS.

1 Preheat the oven to 425°F. Lay the ciabatta slices on a baking sheet and brush with 4 tablespoons of the olive oil. Season with salt and pepper and bake in the oven for 10 minutes until golden brown.

2 Remove from the oven, allow to cool, then grind to coarse crumbs in a food processor. In a large bowl, mix together the tomatoes, cucumber, onion, celery, carrot, and tofu. Add the vinegar and the breadcrumbs, and stir until the vegetables and tofu are coated. Scatter over the basil and chill for about 2 hours. Drizzle with the remaining olive oil just before serving.

nutrition facts	
energy	380 cal
	1566 kJ
protein	12 g
fat	23 g
of which saturated	3 g
carbohydrate	32 g
fiber	2 g
cholesterol	0 mg
sodium	23 mg

mixed **bean** and tofu salad

SERVES 6

FOR THE DRESSING:

Juice of 2 limes

6 Tbsp olive oil

2 Tbsp chopped fresh cilantro

Salt and pepper

FOR THE SALAD:

9 oz firm tofu, cubed

¾ cup green beans, halved

15-oz can red kidney beans, drained and rinsed

15-oz can flageolet beans, drained and rinsed

1 avocado, peeled and sliced

1 bag of mixed salad leaves

AN EXCELLENT SALAD TO SERVE AS PART OF A BUFFET SPREAD, AS ITS TANGY DRESSING PROVIDES A GOOD CONTRAST TO CREAMIER DRESSINGS SUCH AS SOURED CREAM OR MAYONNAISE. IT CAN ALSO BE SERVED AS AN ACCOMPANIMENT TO A MEAT OR FISH MAIN COURSE OR ON ITS OWN WITH PLENTY OF CRUSTY BREAD.

1 For the dressing, shake the ingredients together in a screw-top jar or whisk until combined. Pour over the tofu in a bowl, cover, and chill until required.

2 For the salad, cook the green beans in a pan of boiling water for 5 minutes. Drain and cool under cold water. Pat dry with paper towels and add to the tofu with the kidney beans and flageolet beans. Add the avocado just before serving.

3 Spoon the salad onto a bed of lettuce leaves and serve.

nutrition facts	
energy	320 cal
	1336 kJ
protein	14 g
fat	19 g
of which saturated	3 g
carbohydrate	26 g
fiber	10 g
cholesterol	0 mg
sodium	524 mg

tricolor tofu salad

SERVES 4

½ cup extra-virgin olive oil

2 Tbsp balsamic vinegar

1 garlic clove, peeled and crushed

1 small shallot, peeled and very finely chopped

Salt and freshly ground black pepper

9 oz firm tofu, sliced

2 red bell peppers

4 cups tomatoes

1 ripe avocado

Basil leaves, to garnish

Warm focaccia bread to serve

TOFU REPLACES MOZZARELLA IN THIS POPULAR ITALIAN SALAD. USE THE FULLEST-FLAVORED TOMATOES THAT ARE IN SEASON—CHERRY, PLUM, VINE, OR BEEF WOULD ALL BE SUITABLE.

1 Place the olive oil, vinegar, garlic, shallot, and seasoning in a screw-top jar and shake until thoroughly mixed. Arrange the tofu slices in a shallow dish and pour over the dressing. Cover and chill for 2 hours.

2 Grill the bell peppers until the skins are scorched all over. Place in a bowl, cover, and leave until cool enough to handle, then strip away the skins. Deseed and cut into wedges.

3 Slice, halve, or quarter the tomatoes according to size. Halve the avocado, remove the pit, peel, and slice.

4 Arrange the tofu, tomatoes, peppers, and avocado slices on a large serving platter. Spoon over the dressing remaining in the dish and scatter over basil leaves. Serve at once with warm focaccia bread.

nutrition facts	
energy	330 cal
	1368 kJ
protein	7 g
fat	29 g
of which saturated	5 g
carbohydrate	11 g
fiber	4 g
cholesterol	0 mg
sodium	17 mg

smoked **fish** and **potato** salad with tofu dressing

SERVES 4

FOR THE DRESSING:

2 Tbsp cider vinegar

4 Tbsp sunflower oil

2 Tbsp chopped fresh dill

9 oz soft tofu

Salt and pepper

FOR THE SALAD:

1 lb small new potatoes, cut into halves

2 smoked trout fillets

2 smoked mackerel fillets

4 oz peeled shrimp

1 small red onion, peeled and very finely chopped

1 gherkin, finely chopped

THE DRESSING SHOULD BE THE CONSISTENCY OF HEAVY CREAM SO, DEPENDING ON THE FIRMNESS OF THE TOFU YOU USE, YOU MAY NEED TO BLEND IN EXTRA WATER. MIX THE POTATOES WITH THE DRESSING WHILE THEY ARE STILL WARM SO THAT THEY WILL ABSORB ITS FLAVOR.

1 For the dressing, blend the vinegar, oil, dill, and tofu together until smooth. Add extra water to bring to desired consistency, if necessary. Season to taste.

2 For the salad, cook the potatoes in boiling water until tender. Drain and mix with the dressing. Spoon into a bowl and leave to cool.

3 Remove any skin or bones from the trout and mackerel fillets and break the flesh into bite-size pieces. Tuck among the potatoes in the bowl with the shrimp. Scatter over the chopped onion and gherkin. Cover with plastic wrap, and chill until ready to serve.

nutrition facts	
energy	520 cal
	2151 kJ
protein	26 g
fat	37 g
of which saturated	7 g
carbohydrate	21 g
fiber	1.5 g
cholesterol	128 mg
sodium	652 mg

crab, **mango**, and marinated tofu salad

SERVES 4

9 oz firm tofu, cut into batons

2 large red chiles

2 Tbsp soy sauce

4 Tbsp white wine vinegar

1 tsp brown sugar

1 cup sugar snap peas

1 mango, peeled and flesh chopped

½ cup bean sprouts

½ cup white crabmeat, flaked

1 cup red chard or young spinach leaves

FOR THE DRESSING:

6 Tbsp low-fat soured cream

1 tsp fresh ginger purée

1 Tbsp lime juice

USE WHITE CRABMEAT, PREFERABLY FRESH, WHICH WILL HAVE A BETTER FLAVOR AND TEXTURE THAN CANNED OR FROZEN. RINSE YOUR HANDS THOROUGHLY AFTER HANDLING FRESH CHILES.

1 Place the tofu in a shallow dish. Roast the chiles under a hot broiler until the skins are charred. When cool enough to handle, peel off the skins, remove the seeds, and finely chop the flesh. Mix with the soy sauce, vinegar, and brown sugar, and spoon over the tofu. Set aside for 1 hour.

2 Halve the sugar snap peas and blanch in a pan of boiling water for 30 seconds. Drain and cool under cold water. Add to the tofu with the mango, bean sprouts, and crabmeat.

3 Arrange the red chard or spinach leaves in a shallow serving bowl and pile the tofu mixture in the center, adding any marinade left in the dish. Mix together the soured cream, ginger purée, and lime juice, and drizzle over the salad.

nutrition facts	
energy	225 cal
	1075 kJ
protein	22 g
fat	10 g
of which saturated	3 g
carbohydrate	21 g
fiber	4 g
cholesterol	41 mg
sodium	683 mg

"sushi-style" **exotic fruit** salad

SERVES 4

1 cup long-grain rice

3 Tbsp rice vinegar

½ tsp fresh garlic purée

1 Tbsp mirin (sweet rice wine)

½ tsp fresh lemon grass purée

2 Tbsp sunflower oil

1 Tbsp honey

1 fresh pineapple ring, cut into chunks

4 oz firm tofu, cut into small cubes

1 small mango, peeled and sliced

1 Tbsp Japanese soy sauce

16 green tiger prawns, peeled

4 cleaned squid, sliced

¼ cucumber, chopped

1 kiwi fruit, sliced

ALTHOUGH IN THE WEST WE THINK OF SUSHI AS RICE WRAPPED IN SEAWEED AND VEGETABLES, IN JAPANESE THE WORD SUSHI SIMPLY MEANS SEASONED RICE. THE SEASONING MIX OF RICE VINEGAR, GARLIC, AND MIRIN CAN BE USED TO SEASON ANY TYPE OF RICE.

1 Cook the rice in a pan of simmering water until tender. Drain and tip into a large bowl and, while still hot, stir in the vinegar, garlic purée, mirin, and lemon grass purée. Mix well, then set aside to cool.

2 Heat the sunflower oil in a skillet and add the honey. When hot, sauté the pineapple chunks, tofu, and mango slices in batches over a fairly high heat until lightly caramelized. Remove from the pan and set aside.

3 Add the soy sauce to the pan and sauté the prawns and squid slices for 5 minutes or until the prawns turn pink and the squid is tender.

4 Add the pineapple and seafood mixture, together with the cucumber, kiwi fruit, and any juices from the pan to the rice. Stir well to mix. Transfer to a serving bowl and keep covered until needed.

nutrition facts	
energy	417 cal
	1754 kJ
protein	31 g
fat	9 g
of which saturated	1 g
carbohydrate	53 g
fiber	2 g
cholesterol	315 mg
sodium	444 mg

RIGHT crab, mango, and marinated tofu salad

thai **beef** and tofu salad

SERVES 4

½ tsp fresh lemon grass purée

1 tsp fresh ginger purée

1 Tbsp chopped fresh cilantro

2 Tbsp fish sauce

1 Tbsp chopped fresh mint

Juice of 2 limes

1 tsp brown sugar

2 red chiles, seeded, and finely chopped

9 oz firm tofu, cubed

9 oz fillet or thick rump steak

1 Tbsp coriander seeds, crushed

1 cup baby spinach leaves

1¼ cups mixed green and black seedless grapes, cut into halves

BUY THE BEST-QUALITY STEAK TO ENSURE IT IS VERY TENDER AND TRIM AWAY ANY FAT BEFORE BROILING. LEAVING THE COOKED MEAT TO STAND FOR 15 MINUTES MAKES IT EASIER TO SLICE INTO THIN STRIPS.

1 Mix together the lemon grass and ginger purées, cilantro, fish sauce, mint, lime juice, brown sugar, and chiles. Place the tofu cubes in a bowl and spoon over the mixture, stirring until the tofu is coated. Cover and leave to marinate for 2 hours.

2 Preheat the grill to high. Trim any fat from the steak and roll in the crushed coriander seeds. Grill for 3 to 4 minutes on each side, until well browned but still pink in the center. Set aside for 15 minutes before slicing into thin strips.

3 Rinse the spinach leaves and pat dry with paper towels. Pile into a serving dish and add the grapes and sliced steak. Spoon over the tofu and dressing. Toss lightly and serve.

nutrition facts	
energy	170 cal
	1710 kJ
protein	19 g
fat	6 g
of which saturated	1.5 g
carbohydrate	11 g
fiber	1 g
cholesterol	37 mg
sodium	390 mg

2 appetizers

An entire meal can benefit from an appetizer containing tofu. You can reduce your meat intake, control your calories, and still have the benefits of a tasty first course. Whether hot or cold, tofu appetizers can be tailored to suit your meal. Here, you will find a selection from as far afield as Africa, China, Indonesia, and the Middle East, as well as some traditional and well-loved classic dishes from the West. From burgers and kabobs to fajitas and egg rolls, there is something here to suit every taste.

LEFT Camargue red rice pilaf (page 56)

tabbouleh with tofu, **raisins**, and pine nuts

SERVES 4

¾ cup bulgur wheat

7 Tbsp extra-virgin olive oil

½ cup pine nuts

Grated rind and juice of 1 lemon

2 garlic cloves, peeled and crushed

1 small cucumber

2 tomatoes

4 Tbsp raisins

8 scallions, finely chopped

4 Tbsp chopped fresh flat-leaf parsley

2 Tbsp chopped fresh mint

9 oz firm tofu, cubed

Salt and pepper

AN AROMATIC MIDDLE EASTERN SALAD MADE WITH BULGUR WHEAT AND FRAGRANT FRESH PARSLEY AND MINT. MAKE AHEAD OF TIME AND LEAVE FOR SEVERAL HOURS OR OVERNIGHT BEFORE SERVING TO ALLOW THE FLAVORS TO DEVELOP.

1 Put the bulgur wheat in a large bowl, cover with cold water, and leave to soak for at least 30 minutes. Heat 1 tablespoon of the olive oil in a small skillet and stir-fry the pine nuts briefly until golden. Drain on a plate lined with paper towels.

2 Mix together the remaining olive oil with the lemon juice and garlic. Dice the cucumber, and chop the tomatoes into small pieces.

3 Drain the bulgur wheat in a strainer, shaking out as much excess water as possible. Place in a bowl and add the cucumber, tomatoes, raisins, scallions, parsley, mint, and tofu.

4 Pour over the oil and lemon dressing, and toss well to mix. Add seasoning to taste. Cover the bowl and leave in a cool place for several hours or overnight. Scatter with the pine nuts and grated lemon rind when ready to serve.

nutrition facts	
energy	480 cal
	1996 kJ
protein	11 g
fat	31 g
of which saturated	4 g
carbohydrate	40 g
fiber	2 g
cholesterol	0 mg
sodium	23 mg

glamorgan **sausages**

SERVES 4

3 Tbsp olive oil

1 large leek, trimmed, halved lengthwise and sliced thin

7 oz smoked tofu, grated or finely chopped

2¾ cups potatoes, boiled and mashed

¾ cup strong Cheddar cheese, grated

2 tsp Dijon mustard

3 Tbsp finely chopped fresh parsley

Freshly ground black pepper

4 Tbsp all-purpose flour

THESE VEGETARIAN "SAUSAGES" ARE FLAVORED WITH LEEKS, MUSTARD, AND LOTS OF CHOPPED PARSLEY. LEAVE THEM TO CHILL IN THE REFRIGERATOR FOR SEVERAL HOURS BEFORE COOKING SO THEY HAVE TIME TO FIRM UP.

1 Heat 1 tablespoon of the olive oil in a pan, add the leek, and sauté until softened. Cool, then transfer to a bowl and add the tofu, potatoes, cheese, mustard, parsley, and plenty of freshly ground black pepper. Stir well until mixed, then shape into eight good-size sausages. Put on a plate and chill for at least 1 hour before cooking.

2 Roll the sausages in the flour. Heat the remaining olive oil in a nonstick skillet and cook the sausages until golden brown on all sides. Alternatively, brush with the oil and grill on an aluminum foil-lined rack.

3 Serve with roast chicken, burgers, or steak, or a mixed salad for a vegetarian dish.

nutrition facts	
energy	290 cal
	1197 kJ
protein	12 g
fat	17 g
of which saturated	5 g
carbohydrate	22 g
fiber	2 g
cholesterol	19 mg
sodium	135 mg

rice **egg** rolls with smoked tofu and **sugar snap peas**

SERVES 4

1 cup tiny broccoli florets

1 large carrot, cut into matchsticks

2 Tbsp vegetable oil

½ cup sugar snap peas, cut into halves

4 oz smoked tofu, cut into batons

2 Tbsp soy sauce

1 Tbsp rice vinegar

1 tsp sesame oil

1 small bunch of cilantro leaves, shredded

12 rice flour pancakes

Hoisin or plum dipping sauce to serve

THESE EGG ROLLS CAN BE EATEN COLD OR PLACED IN A STEAMER FOR A FEW MINUTES TO HEAT THEM THROUGH. SERVE WITH A SWEET, SPICY DIP SUCH AS PLUM SAUCE OR HOISIN.

1 Blanch the broccoli florets and carrot sticks in a pan of boiling water for 3 minutes and then drain. Cool by running cold water over them.

2 Heat the oil in a wok or skillet, add the sugar snap peas, broccoli, carrot sticks, and tofu batons, and stir-fry for 5 minutes. Stir in the soy sauce, rice vinegar, sesame oil, and cilantro leaves, and remove from the heat.

3 Dip a rice flour pancake in hot water for a few seconds to soften it. Place on a board and spoon some of the tofu mixture onto one half. Roll the pancake around the filling to make a cone. Repeat with the remaining pancakes and tofu mix until it has all been used.

4 Eat cold or heat through in a steamer for 5 minutes just before serving. Serve accompanied with a dish of hoisin or plum dipping sauce.

nutrition facts	
energy	305 cal
	1274 kJ
protein	11 g
fat	9 g
of which saturated	1 g
carbohydrate	44 g
fiber	3 g
cholesterol	0 mg
sodium	440 mg

potato **pizza**

SERVES 4

3 large potatoes

5 Tbsp olive oil

1 tsp fresh garlic purée

9 oz firm tofu, sliced

2 Tbsp pesto

½ eggplant, sliced thin

1 red onion, peeled and sliced thin

½ cup chèvre (goat cheese log), sliced

Freshly ground black pepper

AN EXCELLENT RECIPE FOR USING UP LEFTOVER ROOT VEGETABLES—CARROTS, POTATOES, PARSNIP, AND RUTABAGA CAN ALL BE MASHED TOGETHER TO MAKE THE BASE.

1 Peel the potatoes and cut into even-size pieces. Cook in a pan of boiling water until tender, then drain and mash with 2 tablespoons olive oil and the garlic.

2 Preheat the oven to 425°F. Spoon the potato onto a baking sheet and press out into a 12-in round. Arrange the tofu slices over the potato.

3 Mix 1 tablespoon olive oil with the pesto and brush over the tofu. Arrange the eggplant, onion, and chèvre slices on top, and brush with the remaining olive oil. Season with black pepper and bake in the oven for 15 to 20 minutes.

nutrition facts	
energy	430 cal
	1790 kJ
protein	14 g
fat	23 g
of which saturated	7 g
carbohydrate	34 g
fiber	4 g
cholesterol	0 mg
sodium	193 mg

mushroom roquefort and tofu strudel

SERVES 4

2 Tbsp olive oil

1 onion, peeled and finely sliced

1 head of fennel, chopped

3 cups mixed mushrooms (such as oyster, chestnut, shiitake), chopped

9 oz firm tofu, cut into small dice

4 red bell peppers, seeded and quartered

2 Tbsp chopped fresh parsley

¾ cup Roquefort cheese, crumbled

¼ cup chopped walnuts

Salt and pepper

8 sheets of phyllo pastry

Extra olive oil, for brushing

1 tsp cumin seeds

SERVE THE STRUDEL WITH A SPICED TOMATO SAUCE, WHICH IS EASY TO MAKE BY STIRRING A TEASPOON (OR MORE IF YOU LIKE THINGS HOT!) OF CHILI PASTE INTO A STORE-BOUGHT PASTA SAUCE.

1 Heat the olive oil in a large skillet, add the onion and fennel, and cook for 5 minutes. Stir in the chopped mushrooms and tofu, and cook for 10 more minutes. Remove from the heat and set aside to cool.

2 Line a broiler pan with aluminum foil and arrange the pepper quarters on it, skin side up. Broil until the skins char, tip the bell peppers into a bowl, and cover with a plate. Leave for 10 minutes then pull off the skins.

3 Drain the mushroom mixture, stir in the parsley, Roquefort, and walnuts, and season.

4 Overlap four of the phyllo sheets on a greased baking sheet, brushing each sheet with a little olive oil. Spoon half the mushroom mixture down the center, leaving enough space around the edge to fold the phyllo sheets up. Arrange the pepper quarters on top, then spoon on the rest of the mushroom mixture. Cover with three of the remaining phyllo sheets, brushing them with olive oil and tucking them under the strudel base to seal them.

5 Cut the last phyllo sheet into ribbons, brush with oil, and arrange over the top in frills to decorate. Scatter the cumin seeds over the strudel. Bake the strudel for 40 minutes or until golden and crisp. Serve hot.

nutrition facts	
energy	410 cal
	170 kJ
protein	17 g
fat	26 g
of which saturated	8 g
carbohydrate	29 g
fiber	6 g
cholesterol	26 mg
sodium	251 mg

mushroom, leek, and tofu quiche

THE PASTRY IN THIS RECIPE IS QUITE SOFT SO, IF YOU FIND IT DIFFICULT TO ROLL, PRESS IT INTO THE PAN WITH YOUR FINGERTIPS, PUSHING TOGETHER ANY CRACKS TO SEAL THEM.

SERVES 8

FOR THE RICH SHORTCRUST PASTRY:

¼ cup butter

¼ cup white vegetable fat

2¼ cups all-purpose flour

2 large egg yolks

FOR THE FILLING:

2 Tbsp olive oil

2 medium leeks, washed and sliced thin

6 cups mixed mushrooms (button, open, oyster, shiitake)

¾ cup blue cheese, such as Stilton or Roquefort

1 Tbsp chopped fresh tarragon

9 oz firm tofu

3 large eggs

½ cup milk

½ cup grated Gruyère cheese

Freshly ground black pepper

Chopped fresh tarragon and black pepper, to garnish

Red chard, to serve

1 For the pastry, blend the fats into the flour. Beat the egg yolks with 3 tablespoons of cold water and stir in. Press the dough together with your fingers and knead lightly until smooth, then wrap in wax paper and chill for 1 hour.

2 Roll out the pastry and line a 9-in round flan dish, 1½ inches deep. Leave to chill while you prepare the filling.

3 For the filling, heat the oil in a large skillet, add the leeks, and cook for 5 minutes. Add the mushrooms and cook for 10 minutes or until softened. Allow to cool.

4 Preheat the oven to 375°F. Stand the pastry case on a cookie sheet and spoon in the leeks and mushrooms, using a slotted spoon so any excess liquid remains in the pan. Crumble over the blue cheese and add the tarragon.

5 Liquidize the tofu, eggs, and milk until smooth and pour into the case. Scatter over the Gruyère and season with black pepper.

6 Bake for 45 to 50 minutes until the quiche is golden and the filling has set. Garnish with fresh tarragon and black pepper and serve with a salad of red chard.

nutrition facts	
energy	385 cal
	1606 kJ
protein	14 g
fat	26 g
of which saturated	11 g
carbohydrate	26 g
fiber	2 g
cholesterol	177 mg
sodium	220 mg

boureks with a tahini and parsley dip

SERVES 4

2 Tbsp olive oil

2 shallots, peeled and finely chopped

1 medium carrot, grated

1 medium zucchini, grated

1 cup mushrooms, chopped

9 oz smoked tofu, finely chopped

6 sheets phyllo pastry

Sunflower oil, for brushing

2 Tbsp sesame or cumin seeds

FOR THE DIP:

1 Tbsp olive oil

1 Tbsp tahini

1 Tbsp chopped flat-leaf parsley

1 clove garlic, crushed

1 tsp chili powder

Toasted sesame seeds

Salt and pepper

Shredded vegetables, such as carrots, zucchini, radish, scallions, and lemon wedges, to garnish

THESE CRISP NORTH AFRICAN PASTRIES ARE FILLED WITH MIXED VEGETABLES AND SMOKED TOFU AND SERVED WITH A SESAME-FLAVORED DIP.

1 Heat the olive oil in a pan and sauté the shallots until softened. Add the carrot, zucchini, and mushrooms, and cook for 5 minutes. Turn up the heat to allow any excess liquid to bubble and evaporate. Stir in the tofu and leave to cool.

2 Cut one sheet of phyllo pastry in half lengthwise and brush lightly with sunflower oil. Spoon a little vegetable mixture at one end and fold the corner of the pastry over to cover it. Continue folding up the pastry length, sealing the final fold with a little oil. Repeat with the remaining pastry and filling until you have made 12 parcels.

3 Preheat the oven to 400°F. Place the boureks on a greased cookie sheet and brush with sunflower oil. Sprinkle with the sesame or cumin seeds and bake for 15 to 20 minutes.

4 For the dip, mix together the ingredients and serve with the hot boureks. Garnish with crisp shredded vegetables and lemon wedges if you like.

nutrition facts	
energy	215 cal
	1884 kJ
protein	4.5 g
fat	16 g
of which saturated	2 g
carbohydrate	13 g
fiber	2 g
cholesterol	0 mg
sodium	10 mg

couscous-stuffed **tomatoes** with smoked tofu and **tuna**

SERVES 6

6 large beefsteak tomatoes

1 Tbsp olive oil

1 garlic clove, peeled and crushed

3 scallions, chopped

⅔ cup couscous

A few saffron threads

1¼ cups fish broth

1 tsp tomato paste

5 oz smoked tofu, finely diced

4-oz can of tuna in brine, drained and flaked

Black pepper

CHOOSE LARGE, EVEN-SIZE BEEF TOMATOES THAT ARE RIPE BUT STILL FIRM FOR THIS DELICIOUS AND HEALTHY DISH.

1 Cut the tops off the tomatoes and scoop out the pulp and seeds with a teaspoon, taking care not to split the skins. Sieve the pulp and reserve, discarding the seeds. Stand the tomatoes upside down on a plate to drain.

2 Heat the oil in a skillet and sauté the garlic and scallions until soft. Add the couscous, saffron, and all but 2 tablespoons of the broth. Mix the tomato paste with the sieved pulp and stir in. Cover the pan and simmer for 10 to 15 minutes until the couscous has swollen and absorbed the liquid, stirring occasionally.

3 Remove from the heat, stir in the smoked tofu and tuna, and season with pepper. Preheat the oven to 350°F.

4 Spoon the filling into the tomato shells, packing down firmly. Stand the tomatoes in a shallow baking pan and replace tops. Spoon over the reserved broth and bake uncovered for 15 to 20 minutes until the tomatoes are tender but not falling apart. Serve hot.

nutrition facts	
energy	125 cal
	515 kJ
protein	9 g
fat	4 g
of which saturated	0.5 g
carbohydrate	15 g
fiber	2 g
cholesterol	9 mg
sodium	192 mg

bang bang **chicken** and tofu

SERVES 4

5 Tbsp crunchy peanut butter

1 tsp sweet chili sauce

1 Tbsp dark soy sauce

¼ cup light olive oil

Few drops of toasted sesame oil

Juice of 1 lime

1 medium carrot, cut into matchsticks

1 bunch of scallions, sliced thin

1½ cups cooked chicken, shredded

9 oz firm tofu cut into batons

Lime wedges, to serve

IF THE PEANUT DRESSING IS TOO THICK, ADD A LITTLE WARM WATER. THIS RECIPE COMES FROM THE SICHUAN REGION OF CHINA WHERE IT IS KNOWN AS BON BON CHICKEN BECAUSE THE MEAT IS HIT WITH A STICK (BON) TO TENDERIZE IT.

1 Place the peanut butter, chili sauce, and soy sauce in a food processor and blend for a few seconds until combined. With the motor running, gradually drizzle the olive oil down the feeder tube. When all the olive oil has been added, add the sesame oil and lime juice, and blend until evenly mixed in. If you do not have a food processor, beat the peanut butter, chili, and soy sauces together in a bowl, then slowly whisk in the olive oil, sesame oil, and lime juice.

2 Place the carrot sticks and scallions into small heaped piles on the serving plates. Divide the chicken and tofu among them, and spoon over the peanut sauce. Serve with lime wedges to squeeze over.

nutrition facts	
energy	440 cal
	1835 kJ
protein	26 g
fat	35 g
of which saturated	6 g
carbohydrate	6 g
fiber	2 g
cholesterol	48 mg
sodium	34 mg

baked potatoes with chili bean tofu

SERVES 4

4 large baking potatoes

1 Tbsp sunflower oil

4 unsmoked bacon slices, chopped

2 shallots, peeled and chopped

2 tsp chili powder

1 green bell pepper, seeded and chopped

1½ cups button mushrooms, cut into quarters

9 oz firm tofu, frozen, defrosted, and coarsely grated

14-oz can chopped tomatoes

2 Tbsp tomato paste

14-oz can kidney beans, drained and rinsed

Salt and pepper

Frisée salad leaves, to serve

ADD EXTRA CHILI POWDER IF YOU LIKE THINGS HOT, OR SUBSTITUTE A MILDER SPICE SUCH AS PAPRIKA IF YOU DON'T.

1 Preheat the oven to 400°F. Prick the potato skins several times, place on a cookie sheet, and bake for about 1 hour or until tender.

2 Meanwhile, heat the oil in a large pan and cook the bacon and shallots over a fairly high heat for 5 minutes until lightly browned. Lower the heat, stir in the chili powder, bell pepper, and mushrooms, and cook for 5 more minutes, stirring frequently. Add the grated tofu, tomatoes, tomato paste, and kidney beans, and season to taste. Simmer uncovered for 15 minutes until the sauce reduces and thickens, stirring occasionally.

3 When the potatoes are done, remove from the oven and cut a deep cross in the top of each one. Press firmly to open up the crosses and place potatoes on serving plates. Spoon over the sauce and serve with frisée salad leaves.

nutrition facts	
energy	440 cal
	1860 kJ
protein	25 g
fat	6 g
of which saturated	1 g
carbohydrate	76 g
fiber	11 g
cholesterol	5 mg
sodium	893 mg

roasted bell peppers with anchovies and tofu

SERVES 4

2 large red bell peppers

2 large yellow or orange bell peppers

12 cherry tomatoes, cut into halves

16 black olives

9 oz firm tofu, cut into ½-in cubes

½ cup pine nuts, toasted

1 large garlic clove, peeled and sliced thin

8 anchovy fillets

1 Tbsp shredded basil leaves

2 Tbsp extra-virgin olive oil

Freshly ground black pepper

DON'T REMOVE THE STALKS WHEN YOU PREPARE THE PEPPERS SO THAT THEY KEEP THEIR SHAPE BETTER DURING COOKING.

1 Preheat the oven to 400°F. Cut the peppers in half lengthwise, cutting through the stalks, and remove the cores and seeds. Place pepper halves in a shallow baking pan, cut sides up.

2 Divide the cherry tomato halves, olives, tofu, pine nuts, and garlic slices among the peppers. Chop the anchovies and scatter over with the shredded basil. Drizzle with the olive oil and season well with freshly ground black pepper.

3 Bake in the oven for 30 minutes or until the peppers are tender. Serve hot with thick slices of hot French bread spread with garlic purée and drizzled with olive oil, then baked in the oven until golden and crisp.

nutrition facts	
energy	300 cal
	1220 kJ
protein	11 g
fat	21 g
of which saturated	2 g
carbohydrate	16 g
fiber	5 g
cholesterol	0 mg
sodium	602 mg

jumbo shrimp with tarragon, mustard and tofu sauce

SERVES 4

16 jumbo shrimp, peeled and deveined

3 Tbsp maple syrup

2 Tbsp rice vinegar

1 tsp fresh lemon grass purée

FOR THE SAUCE:

9 oz firm tofu

½ cup orange juice

1 tsp whole-grain mustard

1 Tbsp chopped fresh tarragon

Salt and pepper

PEEL THE SHRIMP, LEAVING ON THE TAILS, AND SLIT OPEN THE BACK OF EACH ONE TO REMOVE THE BLACK THREAD RUNNING DOWN IT. THE SHRIMP CAN BE LEFT COVERED IN THE REFRIGERATOR TO MARINATE AND THEN GRILLED WHEN NEEDED.

1 Thread the shrimp onto four skewers and place side by side in a shallow dish. Mix together the maple syrup, rice vinegar, and lemon grass purée, and spoon over the shrimp. Cover and leave in the refrigerator to marinate for 3 to 4 hours.

2 For the sauce, liquidize the tofu, orange juice, mustard, and tarragon together, or mash the tofu and whisk in the other ingredients. Spoon into a small pan and season to taste.

3 Lift the shrimp from the marinade and broil or barbecue for about 5 minutes until they turn pink. Stir any marinade left in the dish into the tofu sauce and heat gently without letting it boil.

4 Serve the shrimp skewers on a bed of rice with the sauce spooned over or alongside.

nutrition facts	
energy	200 cal
	852 kJ
protein	32 g
fat	3 g
of which saturated	0.5 g
carbohydrate	11 g
fiber	0 g
cholesterol	290 mg
sodium	300 mg

pan-fried glazed salmon and tofu

SERVES 4

1 lb salmon fillet, skinned and cut into strips

9 oz firm tofu, cut into batons

3 Tbsp light soy sauce

1 tsp sesame oil

Juice of 1 lime

2 tsp liquid honey

1 tsp brown sugar

2 Tbsp sunflower oil

2 carrots, sliced thin

1 celery rib, sliced

1 yellow bell pepper, seeded and sliced thin

½ cup bean sprouts, rinsed

1 green chile, seeded and finely chopped

TO KEEP THE SALMON SUCCULENT, COOK IT BRIEFLY OVER A FAIRLY HIGH HEAT SO THAT IT JUST BROWNS ON THE OUTSIDE. TURN THE PIECES GENTLY TO BROWN BOTH SIDES.

1 Place the salmon and tofu in a shallow dish. Mix together the soy sauce, sesame oil, lime juice, honey, and brown sugar, and pour over. Cover and leave in a cool place to marinate for 1 to 2 hours. Drain the salmon and tofu and reserve the marinade.

2 Heat the sunflower oil in a large skillet or wok, add the salmon and tofu, and cook quickly over a brisk heat until browned. Carefully remove from the pan and keep warm.

3 Stir-fry the carrots, celery, and bell pepper in the same pan for 5 minutes. Add the bean sprouts and chile, and stir-fry for 2 more minutes, pour the marinade over the vegetables, and toss together for 1 minute.

4 Divide the vegetables among four plates, and spoon the salmon and tofu on top. Serve at once.

nutrition facts	
energy	360 cal
	1500 kJ
protein	30 g
fat	22 g
of which saturated	3 g
carbohydrate	11 g
fiber	2.5 g
cholesterol	56 mg
sodium	717 mg

tomato **rice** with **smoked bacon**, chicken livers, and tofu

SERVES 4

1 Tbsp sunflower oil

1 bunch of scallions, trimmed and chopped

1 cup long-grain rice

2¾ cups chicken broth

6 slices smoked bacon, cut into halves

12 oz chicken livers, cut into small pieces

9 oz firm tofu, cubed

6 medium tomatoes, cut into halves

2 Tbsp liquid honey

1 Tbsp sweet soy sauce

Salt and black pepper

2 Tbsp snipped chives

IT IS IMPORTANT NOT TO OVERCOOK THE CHICKEN LIVERS AS, LIKE ALL LIVER, THEY WILL BECOME DRY AND TOUGH. THEY ARE READY WHEN STILL SLIGHTLY PINK IN THE MIDDLE.

1 Preheat the oven to 400°F. Heat the oil in a large skillet and sauté the scallions until softened. Stir in the rice and cook for 1 minute, then add half the broth, and simmer for 20 to 25 minutes (check the cooking instructions on the package of rice), gradually adding as much of the remaining broth as necessary until the rice is cooked.

2 Stretch the halved bacon slices with the back of a knife and roll up. Place the bacon rolls, chicken livers, and tofu on one side of a shallow roasting pan, and the tomato halves on the other. Mix together the honey and soy sauce, and brush over the bacon, chicken livers, and tofu. Cook in the oven for 20 minutes.

3 When the rice is cooked, scoop the tomato flesh out of the skins, roughly chop, and stir into the rice. Season with salt and pepper.

4 Serve the rice with the bacon, chicken livers, and tofu, sprinkled with the chives.

nutrition facts	
energy	590 cal
	2483 kJ
protein	33 g
fat	24 g
of which saturated	7 g
carbohydrate	62 g
fiber	2 g
cholesterol	369 mg
sodium	1253 mg

layered tofu and **vegetable terrine**

SERVES 8

About 10 large spinach leaves

FOR THE TOFU LAYER:

1 small red bell pepper, seeded, and finely chopped

9 oz firm tofu

1 tsp Dijon mustard

1 medium egg, beaten

¼ cup all-purpose flour

½ cup low-fat Cheddar cheese, grated

Salt and pepper

½ cup green beans, cooked

FOR THE CARROT LAYER:

1⅓ cups grated carrots

2 Tbsp orange juice

2 medium eggs, beaten

¼ cup all-purpose flour

FOR THE BROCCOLI LAYER:

1½ cups broccoli, cooked and chopped

½ cup curd cheese

1 medium egg, beaten

1 Tbsp all-purpose flour

SERVE THIS WARM WITH A SPICY TOMATO SAUCE AND NEW POTATOES, OR COLD WITH A SALAD. IF SERVING WARM, LEAVE IT TO STAND FOR 10 MINUTES BEFORE TURNING OUT. IF SERVING COLD, ALLOW IT TO COOL WITH A WEIGHT ON TOP, THEN CHILL UNTIL IT IS READY TO SERVE.

1 Rinse the spinach leaves and cut away any tough stalks. Cook in a very little water until wilted. Drain, cover with cold water, then drain again.

2 Grease a 2-pound loaf pan and line the base with wax paper. Line the pan with the spinach leaves, saving one or two for the top.

3 To make the tofu layer, blanch the chopped bell pepper in a pan of boiling water for 1 minute. Drain and cool under cold water. Purée the tofu, mustard, egg, and flour together, then stir in the cheese and seasoning. Spoon into the pan and lay the beans on top running lengthwise.

4 To make the carrot layer, mix the ingredients together and season to taste. Spoon into the pan over the beans.

5 To make the broccoli layer, mix the ingredients together, season, and spoon into the pan. Cover with the reserved spinach leaves and fold over any overlapping the pan.

6 Preheat the oven to 350°F. Cover the terrine with wax paper and wrap the pan in aluminum foil. Stand in a shallow pan (in case of leaks during baking) and bake in the oven for 1¼ hours. Serve warm or cold.

nutrition facts	
energy	192 cal
	799 kJ
protein	11 g
fat	12 g
of which saturated	5 g
carbohydrate	10 g
fiber	2 g
cholesterol	132 mg
sodium	134 mg

salmon and tofu cakes with a spiced sesame dip

MAKES 20 CAKES

9 oz salmon fillet, skinned

1 tsp fresh ginger purée

1 tsp ground cumin

1 green chile, seeded, and chopped

9 oz firm tofu, frozen, defrosted, and grated

1 small egg, beaten

1 Tbsp all-purpose flour

2 Tbsp chopped fresh cilantro

Vegetable oil, for shallow frying

FOR THE DIPPING SAUCE:

4 Tbsp dark soy sauce

1 Tbsp hoisin sauce

1 tsp chili sauce

2 tsp sesame seeds

Lime wedges, to serve

FREEZING FIRM TOFU AND THEN DEFROSTING MAKES IT FIRM ENOUGH TO GRATE. FREEZE THE TOFU IN ITS PACKAGE THE DAY BEFORE NEEDED AND DEFROST OVERNIGHT IN THE FRIDGE. THESE CAKES CAN BE SERVED AS A LIGHT MEAL OR AS AN APPETIZER WITH DRINKS.

1 Cut the salmon fillet into chunks and place in a food processor with the ginger purée, cumin, and chile. Process for about 30 seconds until finely chopped but not reduced to a mush. Alternatively, finely chop the salmon with a sharp knife and mix with the purée, cumin, and very finely chopped chile.

2 Transfer to a bowl and mix in the grated tofu, beaten egg, flour, and cilantro. Cover and chill for 2 to 3 hours to firm the mixture.

3 With floured hands, shape into 20 small, flat cakes. Shallow fry in hot vegetable oil in batches until golden brown on both sides. Drain and serve at once or allow to cool and, when ready to serve, spread the cakes out on a cookie sheet and reheat for 10 minutes in a 400°F oven.

4 For the dipping sauce, mix together the soy, hoisin, and chili sauces. Transfer to a shallow bowl and sprinkle in the sesame seeds. Serve with the fish cakes and lime wedges.

nutrition facts	
energy	62 cal
	260 kJ
protein	4 g
fat	5 g
of which saturated	1 g
carbohydrate	1 g
fiber	0 g
cholesterol	17 mg
sodium	225 mg

oven-baked cheesed **potato** skins with tofu and **sun-dried tomato** dip

SERVES 4

4 large potatoes, for baking
2 Tbsp olive oil
1 cup grated pecorino cheese
½ tsp mustard powder
Salt and pepper

FOR THE DIP:
9 oz soft tofu
2 tsp sun-dried tomato purée
2 Tbsp ketchup
¼ tsp smoked paprika

SMOKED PAPRIKA IS SIMILAR TO NORMAL PAPRIKA BUT HAS A WARM, CHAR-GRILLED SMOKINESS, BECAUSE THE RED PEPPERS USED TO MAKE IT ARE SMOKED IMMEDIATELY AFTER PICKING. SMOKED PAPRIKA IS AVAILABLE FROM LARGER SUPERMARKETS.

1 Preheat the oven to 350°F. Slit the potatoes around the center with a sharp knife and bake for 1¼ hours, or for about 20 minutes on full power in a microwave oven until tender when pierced with a skewer. Allow to cool.

2 Cut the potatoes in half and scoop out the flesh (use the flesh for another recipe), leaving a ¼-inch layer inside the skins. Brush the skins with the olive oil and cut each half-skin into four. Place on a cookie sheet, skin side down. Mix together the cheese, mustard powder, and seasoning, and sprinkle over the potato skins.

3 Preheat the oven to 375°F and bake for 20 to 25 minutes or until the skins are crisp.

4 For the dip, mash or liquidize the tofu with the sun-dried tomato purée and ketchup. Spoon into a small bowl and dust with the smoked paprika. Serve the potato skins with the dip.

nutrition facts	
energy	370 cal
	1521 kJ
protein	20 g
fat	17 g
of which saturated	6 g
carbohydrate	36 g
fiber	3 g
cholesterol	25 mg
sodium	307 mg

Camargue **red rice** pilaf

SERVES 4

1 cup Camargue red rice

2 cups vegetable broth

2 Tbsp sunflower oil

9 oz firm tofu, cut into batons

½ cup shiitake mushrooms, cut into quarters

2 Tbsp light soy sauce

7 oz peeled shrimp

4 oz smoked mussels

1 cup frozen peas

½ cup coconut milk

Freshly ground black pepper

Chives, to garnish

THE UNIQUE RED-BROWN RICE THAT GROWS IN THE WETLANDS OF THE CAMARGUE REGION OF SOUTHERN FRANCE HAS A DISTINCTIVE NUTTY FLAVOR AND MAKES AN EXCELLENT PILAF OR RICE SALAD.

1 Put the rice and broth in a saucepan and simmer for 30 to 35 minutes until the rice is tender. When the rice is almost ready, heat the oil in a deep skillet, add the tofu and mushrooms, and cook for 5 minutes, stirring occasionally. Add the soy sauce and cook for another couple of minutes until most of the sauce has been absorbed by the tofu and mushrooms.

2 Drain the rice and stir into the pan with the shrimp, mussels, peas, and coconut milk. Season with pepper and cook for 5 minutes or until the seafood and peas are heated through. Garnish with lengths of fresh chive.

nutrition facts	
energy	440 cal
	1835 kJ
protein	28 g
fat	15 g
of which saturated	5 g
carbohydrate	44 g
fiber	1.5 g
cholesterol	55 mg
sodium	1461 mg

seared **scallops** with tofu **curry** mayonnaise

SERVES 4

12 scallops

1 tsp lemon grass purée

1 tsp chili purée

1 tsp garlic purée

1 Tbsp dry sherry

FOR THE TOFU MAYONNAISE:

4 Tbsp low-calorie mayonnaise

4 oz firm tofu

1 tsp curry paste

1 Tbsp fresh lemon juice

Vegetable rice, to serve

USING STORE-BOUGHT JARS OF PURÉED FRESH SPICES SUCH AS GINGER, LEMON GRASS, AND CHILI SAVES ON PREPARATION TIME AS THEY CAN BE ADDED STRAIGHT TO A DISH. ONCE OPENED, STORE THE JARS IN THE REFRIGERATOR AND USE BY THE RECOMMENDED DATE.

1 Place the scallops in a shallow dish. Mix together the lemon grass and the chili and garlic purées with the sherry, and spread over the scallops. Cover and leave in a cool place to marinate for 1 hour.

2 For the mayonnaise, liquidize the ingredients together until smooth or mash the tofu and beat in the mayonnaise, curry paste, and lemon juice. Spoon into a serving dish, cover, and chill until required.

3 Heat a heavy nonstick skillet or ridged broiler pan until very hot. Add the scallops and cook for 5 minutes, turning over once. Serve the scallops with the mayonnaise and accompany with vegetable rice.

nutrition facts	
energy	130 cal
	530 kJ
protein	14 g
fat	6 g
of which saturated	0 g
carbohydrate	3 g
fiber	0 g
cholesterol	27 mg
sodium	251 mg

tofu and **chipolata Yorkshires**
with shallot gravy

SERVES 4

FOR THE BATTER:

½ cup all-purpose flour

1 large egg

¾ cup milk

FOR THE FILLING:

6 oz firm tofu, cubed

1 Tbsp olive oil

2 tsp balsamic vinegar

2 tsp chopped fresh thyme
leaves

2 tsp white vegetable fat

4 chipolata sausages, cut into
halves

6 shallots, peeled and thinly
sliced

¾ cup beer or stout

1 Tbsp molasses

1 vegetable bouillon cube

1 Tbsp tomato paste

Peas or mashed potatoes, to
serve

IF YOU DO NOT HAVE A FOUR-CUP YORKSHIRE
PUDDING TRAY, USE A 7-INCH SQUARE SHALLOW
PAN, DOUBLE THE QUANTITY OF FLOUR AND MILK,
AND BAKE FOR 40 TO 45 MINUTES.

1 To make the batter, sift the flour into a bowl and add the egg. Mix
with a wooden spoon, gradually adding the milk until you have a
smooth batter. Set aside for 1 hour.

2 To make the filling, place the tofu in a shallow dish and spoon over
the olive oil and vinegar. Scatter over half the thyme and set aside for
30 minutes.

3 Preheat the oven to 425°F. Divide the vegetable fat among the four
cups of a Yorkshire pudding tray. Place in the oven until melted and
very hot. Lift the tofu from the dish with a draining spoon and divide
among the cups with the halved chipolatas. Pour over the batter and
return to the oven. Bake for 15 to 20 minutes until well risen and
golden brown.

4 Meanwhile, place the shallots, remaining thyme, beer or stout,
molasses, bouillon cube, ¾ cup water and tomato paste in a pan and
bring to a boil. Simmer for 10 minutes,
stirring occasionally. Serve the
Yorkshires as soon as they are ready
with the gravy spooned over them.
Serve with peas or mashed potatoes.

nutrition facts	
energy	200 cal
	854 kJ
protein	9 g
fat	10 g
of which saturated	3 g
carbohydrate	19 g
fiber	1 g
cholesterol	69 mg
sodium	346 mg

chinese egg rolls with hoisin-glazed tofu

SERVES 4

9 oz firm tofu, cut into small cubes

2 Tbsp hoisin sauce

1 Tbsp light soy sauce

1 tsp fresh ginger purée

8 shiitake mushrooms, chopped

½ cup bean sprouts

6 scallions, finely chopped

4 oz cooked peeled shrimp

1 Tbsp cornstarch

20 egg roll wrappers

Oil for shallow-frying

Chili sauce, plum sauce, or rice vinegar, to serve

FROZEN EGG ROLL WRAPPERS ARE AVAILABLE FROM CHINESE FOOD STORES AND COME IN PACKETS OF AROUND 20 SHEETS. DEFROST THE BLOCK OF SHEETS BEFORE PEELING OFF EACH ONE VERY CAREFULLY SO AS NOT TO TEAR IT. COVER THE ONES YOU ARE NOT USING WITH A DAMP CLOTH TO PREVENT THEM FROM DRYING OUT.

1 Place the tofu in a mixing bowl. Mix together the hoisin, soy sauce, and ginger purée, and spoon over the tofu, stirring until coated. Set aside for 30 minutes.

2 Add the mushrooms, bean sprouts, scallions, and shrimp to the tofu, and mix in.

3 Mix the cornstarch with a little cold water to make a paste. Lay an egg roll wrapper on a board, spoon a little tofu mixture diagonally across the center, fold over the ends of the wrapper loosely, and roll up into a cigar shape. Seal the edges by brushing with a little of the cornstarch paste. Repeat with the remaining wrappers and filling.

4 Shallow-fry the egg rolls in three or four batches in a little hot vegetable oil for about 5 minutes or until golden brown on all sides. Drain on paper towels and serve hot with a dip of chili sauce, plum sauce, or rice vinegar.

nutrition facts	
energy	350 cal
	1475 kJ
protein	16 g
fat	15 g
of which saturated	2 g
carbohydrate	38 g
fiber	2 g
cholesterol	49 mg
sodium	583 mg

tofu paneer with **peas** and **cilantro**

SERVES 4

2 Tbsp vegetable oil

¾ cup paneer, cut into 1-in cubes

9 oz firm tofu, cut into 1-in cubes

1 large onion, peeled and sliced thin

2 garlic cloves, peeled and crushed

2 tsp fresh ginger purée

1 tsp ground turmeric

1 Tbsp ground coriander

1 tsp fresh chili purée

1 tsp ground cumin

3½ cups frozen peas

8-oz can chopped tomatoes

2 Tbsp chopped fresh cilantro

PANEER IS INDIAN CURD CHEESE AND CAN BE FOUND IN LARGER SUPERMARKETS AS WELL AS INDIAN FOOD STORES. AS WITH TOFU, IT ABSORBS OTHER FLAVORS WELL, PARTICULARLY SPICES.

1 Heat the oil in a large skillet, add the paneer and tofu cubes, and sauté for 10 minutes, turning occasionally, until they are golden brown all over. Drain from the pan and set aside.

2 Add the onion to the pan and sauté gently for 10 minutes. Add the garlic, ginger purée, turmeric, coriander, chili, and cumin, and cook for 5 more minutes. Stir in the peas and chopped tomatoes, and return the paneer and tofu cubes to the pan.

3 Simmer for 5 minutes until heated through. Serve at once garnished with the chopped cilantro.

nutrition facts	
energy	190 cal
	800 kJ
protein	15 g
fat	11 g
of which saturated	2 g
carbohydrate	10 g
fiber	2 g
cholesterol	7 mg
sodium	217 mg

glazed **chicken** and tofu skewers

SERVES 4

9 oz firm tofu, frozen, defrosted, and cut into chunks

2 chicken breasts, skinned and cut into chunks

4 Tbsp hot mango chutney

Juice of 1 lime

4 Tbsp plain yogurt

2 Tbsp chopped fresh mint

FOR THE DRESSING:

3 Tbsp plain yogurt

1 Tbsp sunflower oil

1 Tbsp lemon juice

1 Tbsp chopped fresh mint

½ tsp paprika

Lime wedges, radiccio and frisée lettuce, to serve

MILD MANGO CHUTNEY CAN BE USED INSTEAD OF THE HOT VARIETY, IF YOU PREFER. REMOVE ANY FIBROUS PIECES OF FRUIT FROM THE CHUTNEY BEFORE MIXING IT WITH THE OTHER MARINADE INGREDIENTS.

1 Thread the tofu and chicken chunks alternately onto thin skewers. Place side by side in a shallow dish.

2 Mix together the mango chutney, lime juice, yogurt, and mint, and spoon over the skewers, turning them over to coat thoroughly. Cover and leave in a cool place to marinate for several hours or overnight.

3 For the dressing, whisk the ingredients together. Add a little water if too thick. Broil or barbecue the skewers for about 5 to 6 minutes or until the chicken is cooked, turning over once or twice. Serve hot with the yogurt dipping sauce and lime wedges to squeeze over. Serve on a bed of radiccio and frisée lettuce.

nutrition facts	
energy	200 cal
	831 kJ
protein	21 g
fat	9 g
of which saturated	2 g
carbohydrate	9 g
fiber	0 g
cholesterol	44 mg
sodium	267 mg

lamb and tofu **burgers**

SERVES 4

9 oz smoked tofu, finely chopped

9 oz lean ground lamb

2 shallots, peeled and very finely chopped

1 Tbsp sun-dried tomato paste

1 tsp fresh garlic purée

1 Tbsp chopped fresh mint

2 Tbsp sunflower oil

4 hamburger buns, split and toasted

Lettuce leaves and red onion slices, to serve

THESE BURGERS CAN BE COOKED IN A RIDGED GRIDDLE PAN, BARBECUED, OR SHALLOW-FRIED IN A LITTLE SUNFLOWER OIL. YOU CAN SERVE THEM WITH LEAVES AND GARNISH OF YOUR CHOICE.

1 In a large bowl, mix together the tofu, lamb, chopped shallots, tomato paste, garlic purée, and mint. Divide into four and shape into burgers. Chill for 1 hour.

2 Brush the burgers with the oil and cook in a ridged griddle pan for 5 minutes on each side or until done to your liking. Alternatively, fry them in the oil in a heavy pan, skillet, or barbecue.

3 Serve in the burger buns with lettuce, red onion, and relishes of your choice.

nutrition facts	
energy	380 cal
	1588 kJ
protein	25 g
fat	15 g
of which saturated	4 g
carbohydrate	38 g
fiber	1 g
cholesterol	49 mg
sodium	457 mg

cajun **chicken** and tofu **fajitas** with guacamole salsa

SERVES 4

2 boneless chicken breasts, skinned

9 oz firm tofu

1 Tbsp Cajun seasoning

2 Tbsp sunflower oil

1 red onion, peeled and sliced

Juice of 1 lime

4 jalapeño chiles, sliced thin

FOR THE GUACAMOLE SALSA:

1 avocado, peeled and pitted

Juice of ½ lime

1 tomato, finely chopped

1 garlic clove, peeled and crushed

½ tsp chili sauce

8 soft flour tortillas and soured cream, to serve

JARS OF CAJUN SEASONING ARE AVAILABLE FROM SUPERMARKETS BUT YOU CAN SUBSTITUTE A MIXTURE OF MILD OR HOT CHILI POWDER AND GROUND CUMIN IF YOU PREFER.

1 Cut the chicken and tofu into bite-size pieces and sprinkle over the Cajun seasoning to coat. Set aside for 30 minutes.

2 Heat the oil in a large skillet, add the onion, and sauté for 5 minutes. Add the chicken and tofu, and stir-fry over a fairly high heat for 5 more minutes or until golden. Squeeze over the lime juice, add the sliced jalapeños, and cook for 1 to 2 minutes more.

3 While the chicken is cooking, make the salsa. Mash the avocado flesh with the lime juice, stir in the tomato, garlic, and chili sauce.

4 To serve, warm the tortillas according to the package instructions and top each tortilla with the chicken mixture, a spoonful of salsa, and the soured cream. Roll up the tortilla around the filling and serve.

nutrition facts	
energy	270 cal
	1129 kJ
protein	23 g
fat	18 g
of which saturated	3 g
carbohydrate	5 g
fiber	2 g
cholesterol	32 mg
sodium	2 mg

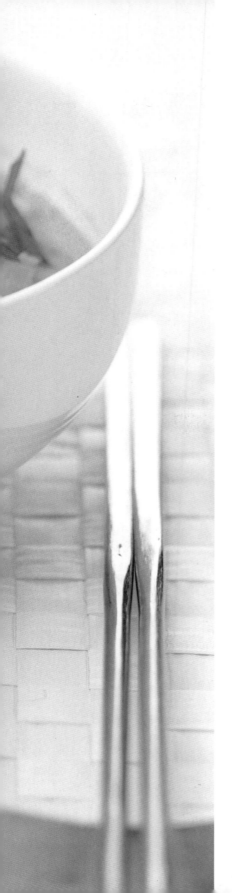

3 main dishes

You will find an excellent selection of tofu main dishes in this section. Spanning a wide variety of cultures and tastes, you can truly explore the versatility of tofu. Broiled, stir-fried, or baked, these dishes will amaze you in their inventive and mouth-watering use of tofu. With a selection of tastes and textures to impress the fussiest eater, these recipes truly show you how to make tofu part of your everyday diet.

LEFT laksa (page 80)

roasted **squash**, tofu, and **apple** tartlets

SERVES 4

8 sheets of phyllo pastry

4 Tbsp sunflower oil

2 red-skinned dessert apples, cored and cut into chunks

Juice of ½ lemon

1 butternut squash, peeled and cut into ¾-in chunks

9 oz firm tofu, cubed

1 red onion, peeled and cut into wedges

2 Tbsp balsamic vinegar

2 Tbsp maple syrup

½ tsp harissa or chili paste

2 Tbsp oyster sauce

Chopped marjoram, to garnish

COVER THE PHYLLO SHEETS WITH PLASTIC WRAP AND A DAMP CLOTH TO PREVENT THEM FROM DRYING OUT BEFORE USE. ROLL UNUSED SHEETS, RETURN THEM TO THE PACKAGE, AND STORE FOR 2 TO 3 DAYS IN THE REFRIGERATOR, OR FREEZE UNTIL NEEDED.

1 Preheat the oven to 400°F. Lay the phyllo sheets on a board and cut them in half. Place four heatproof cups or small pudding containers upsidedown on a baking sheet. Using half the oil, brush a little over the outsides of the cups.

2 Brush the phyllo sheets lightly with oil and layer them, four over each container. Arrange the points at irregular angles and press down gently. Bake for 15 minutes or until golden. Remove from the oven and, when cool enough to handle, lift carefully off the containers and place the right way up on the cookie sheet.

3 Toss the apple chunks with the lemon juice and spread out in a shallow baking pan with the squash, tofu, and onion wedges. Mix together the remaining oil, balsamic vinegar, maple syrup, harissa or chili paste and oyster sauce, and drizzle over the mixture. Turn over to coat the apples, vegetables, and tofu, and roast in the oven for 20 minutes.

4 When almost ready, return the phyllo cases to the oven for a few minutes to heat through. Fill the cases with the roasted mixture (any that won't fit in can be served separately). Garnish with lengths of fresh chive and serve at once with an herbed tomato sauce and mixed leaf salad.

nutrition facts	
energy	340 cal
	1436 kJ
protein	10 g
fat	14 g
of which saturated	1.5 g
carbohydrate	45 g
fiber	5 g
cholesterol	0 mg
sodium	326 mg

penne with chili-roasted tofu and vegetables

SERVES 4

6 Tbsp olive oil

1 tsp chili sauce

1 each red, yellow, and orange bell peppers, seeded and roughly chopped

2 red onions, peeled and cut into wedges

2 zucchini, chopped

1½ cups chestnut mushrooms, cut into quarters

3 garlic cloves, peeled and sliced

9 oz firm tofu, cubed

2 tomatoes, cut into quarters

3 cups penne

2 tsp sun-dried tomato paste

1 Tbsp fennel seeds

CUMIN SEEDS MAKE AN AROMATIC ALTERNATIVE IF YOU CAN'T FIND FENNEL. DIFFERENT COMBINATIONS OF VEGETABLES CAN BE USED, AND YOU CAN ADD OTHERS OF YOUR CHOICE IF YOU PREFER.

1 Preheat the oven to 400°F. Mix 4 tablespoons of the olive oil with the chili sauce and spoon into a shallow roasting pan. Place in the oven until very hot. Add the prepared peppers, onions, zucchini, mushrooms, garlic, and tofu, turning them over with a large spoon to coat with the oil.

2 Roast for 30 minutes, then add the tomatoes and roast for 10 to 15 minutes more or until the vegetables are tender and charred at the edges.

3 About 10 minutes before they are done, cook the penne in a large pan of boiling water until *al dente* (firm to the bite). Mix the rest of the olive oil with the sun-dried tomato paste and toss with the drained penne.

4 Toss the pasta with vegetables and tofu and pile into the serving plates. Scatter over the fennel seeds, and serve.

nutrition facts	
energy	467 cal
	1952 kJ
protein	15 g
fat	21 g
of which saturated	3 g
carbohydrate	57 g
fiber	5 g
cholesterol	0 mg
sodium	58 mg

spaghetti with tofu puttanesca

SERVES 4

2 Tbsp olive oil

1 red bell pepper, seeded and finely chopped

9 oz firm tofu, frozen, defrosted, and grated

3 garlic cloves, peeled and finely chopped

1 large red chile, seeded and finely chopped

3 large plum tomatoes, peeled and chopped

1 Tbsp red pesto

1 Tbsp capers

1¼ cups pitted green olives, roughly chopped

Salt and pepper

12 oz spaghetti

grated Parmesan cheese, to serve

THE CLASSIC PUTTANESCA SAUCE IS NAMED AFTER ROME'S "LADIES OF PLEASURE" AND IS A SPICY MIX OF TOMATOES, ANCHOVIES, AND CAPERS. HERE, I HAVE ADDED BELL PEPPERS AND TOFU TO THE ORIGINAL RECIPE, TURNING IT INTO A MORE SUBSTANTIAL MEAL WITHOUT ADDING MEAT.

1 Heat the oil in a large pan, add the bell pepper, tofu, garlic, and chile, and sauté over a low heat for 10 minutes.

2 Add the tomatoes, pesto, capers, and olives, and season to taste. Simmer for 20 minutes or until the excess liquid from the tomatoes has evaporated and the sauce has reduced and thickened.

3 Meanwhile, cook the spaghetti according to the package instructions until *al dente* (firm to the bite). Drain and divide among four serving bowls. Spoon over the sauce and serve at once, topped with plenty of freshly grated Parmesan cheese.

nutrition facts	
energy	500 cal
	2091 kJ
protein	25 g
fat	16 g
of which saturated	2.5 g
carbohydrate	72 g
fiber	6 g
cholesterol	0 mg
sodium	1003 mg

roasted **vegetable** and tofu couscous with **harissa** sauce

SERVES 4

FOR THE HARISSA SAUCE:

2 red bell peppers

3 large red chiles

2 fat garlic cloves, peeled and chopped

2 tsp cumin seeds

1 Tbsp ground coriander

4 Tbsp olive oil

FOR THE COUSCOUS:

12 baby carrots

3 Tbsp olive oil

1 yellow bell pepper, seeded and cut into chunks

1 eggplant, cut into small pieces

1½ cups chestnut mushrooms, cut into halves

1 red onion, peeled, cut into wedges, and layers separated

½ cup blanched almonds

7 oz smoked tofu, cubed

1¼ cups couscous

½ tsp saffron threads

HARISSA IS A NORTH AFRICAN CHILI SAUCE THAT IS EXCELLENT SERVED WITH PASTA AND RICE DISHES OR WITH ROASTED MEAT AND FISH. ANY THAT IS LEFT OVER CAN BE STORED IN A SCREW-TOP JAR IN THE REFRIGERATOR FOR ABOUT ONE WEEK.

1 For the sauce, broil the peppers and chiles until the skins are scorched all over. Cover, leave to cool, then peel off the skins, deseed, and roughly chop the flesh. Place the peppers, chiles, garlic, cumin, and coriander in a food processor and blend until smooth. Add the olive oil and process again until combined.

2 For the couscous, preheat the oven to 400°F.

3 Blanch the carrots in a pan of boiling water for 5 minutes, then drain. Spoon the olive oil into a shallow roasting pan and place in the oven until very hot. Add all the vegetables and turn them over to coat with the oil.

4 Roast for 20 minutes, then scatter the almonds and tofu cubes among the vegetables, and cook for another 10 to 15 minutes or until the vegetables are tender and browned at the edges.

5 While the vegetables are cooking, put the couscous and saffron threads in a heatproof bowl and pour over boiling water to cover. Cover and leave to stand for 10 minutes or until all the water has been absorbed. Transfer the couscous to a serving dish and fork up the grains. Spoon the vegetable mixture on top and either spoon over warm or cold harissa sauce, or serve it separately.

nutrition facts	
energy	500 cal
	2056 kJ
protein	13 g
fat	30 g
of which saturated	4 g
carbohydrate	46 g
fiber	7 g
cholesterol	0 mg
sodium	28 mg

thai braised tofu with glass **noodles**

SERVES 4

1¼ cups small broccoli florets

1 Tbsp sunflower oil

1 small red bell pepper, seeded and chopped

3 cups shiitake mushrooms, sliced

9 oz firm tofu, cut into 1-in cubes

2 Tbsp creamed coconut, chopped

1½ cups hot chicken broth

1 tsp fresh lemon grass purée

4 Tbsp smooth peanut butter

2 Tbsp fish sauce

2 cups glass noodles

1 tsp sesame oil

ALSO KNOWN AS BEAN THREAD AND CELLOPHANE NOODLES, GLASS NOODLES ARE THIN, OPAQUE WHITE THREADS MADE FROM MUNG BEANS. RICE VERMICELLI CAN BE USED AS A SUBSTITUTE.

1 Blanch the broccoli florets in a pan of boiling water for 3 minutes, then drain. Heat the oil in a large pan, add the bell pepper, mushrooms, and tofu, and sauté for 10 minutes over a low heat.

2 Dissolve the creamed coconut in the broth and stir into the pan with the lemon grass purée, peanut butter, fish sauce, and broccoli, and simmer for 5 minutes. Meanwhile, cut the noodles into short lengths with scissors and place them in a bowl. Pour over boiling water to cover and leave to stand for 5 minutes. Drain and sprinkle with sesame oil.

3 Divide the noodles among four serving bowls and spoon over the braised tofu.

nutrition facts	
energy	440 cal
	1843 kJ
protein	16 g
fat	19 g
of which saturated	6 g
carbohydrate	49 g
fiber	3 g
cholesterol	0 mg
sodium	564 mg

carrot, **fava bean**, and tofu risotto

SERVES 4

1 cup baby carrots, cut into halves lengthwise

¼ cup butter

2 Tbsp olive oil

2 garlic cloves, peeled and finely chopped

9 oz firm tofu, cut into batons

1 cup Arborio rice

¾ cup dry white wine

3½ cups vegetable broth

1¼ cups frozen fava beans

1 Tbsp pesto

⅔ cup freshly grated Parmesan cheese

Salt and pepper

ARBORIO RICE IS BEST FOR RISOTTOS. ITS PLUMP GRAINS ABSORB PLENTY OF LIQUID WHILE COOKING—GIVING IT A DELICIOUSLY CREAMY TEXTURE, WHILE STILL RETAINING A LITTLE "BITE."

1 Cook the carrots in a pan of boiling water for 5 minutes and then drain. Put the pan back on the heat, add half the butter with the oil, and, when melted, add the carrots, garlic, and tofu. Sauté over a low heat for 5 minutes, then set aside.

2 Melt the remaining butter in a large, heavy skillet, add the rice, and stir around the pan for 1 to 2 minutes. Add the wine and boil for 2 minutes to reduce a little.

3 Heat the broth in a pan and keep at a gentle simmer. Add a ladleful of broth to the rice and stir with a wooden spoon until absorbed. Continue adding the hot broth, a ladleful at a time, making sure each addition is absorbed by the rice before adding the next. Cook for about 20 minutes until most of the broth has been added.

4 Stir the carrot and tofu mixture into the rice with the remaining broth and fava beans. Continue to cook, stirring, until the rice is tender. Remove from the heat, stir in the pesto, half the Parmesan, and the seasoning. Cover and leave to stand for 5 minutes, before serving with the remaining Parmesan scattered over it.

nutrition facts	
energy	540 cal
	2261 kJ
protein	18 g
fat	24 g
of which saturated	11 g
carbohydrate	54 g
fiber	4 g
cholesterol	41 mg
sodium	635 mg

salmon, **spinach**, and tofu pie

SERVES 6

4 cups spinach leaves, coarse stalks removed

9 oz firm tofu, cubed

12 oz salmon fillet, skinned and cubed

4 Tbsp rice vinegar

2 Tbsp soy sauce

1 tsp fresh garlic purée

½ tsp English mustard powder

About 9 sheets of phyllo pastry

Sunflower oil, for brushing

1 Tbsp sesame seeds

FROZEN SPINACH COULD BE USED FOR THIS RECIPE BUT ONLY HALF THE QUANTITY GIVEN FOR FRESH SPINACH WILL BE NEEDED. DEFROST FROZEN SPINACH IN A HEAVY SKILLET OVER A LOW HEAT AND LEAVE UNTIL ALL THE EXCESS WATER HAS EVAPORATED SO THE SPINACH IS DRY, STIRRING OCCASIONALLY SO THAT IT DOESN'T STICK TO THE BOTTOM OF THE PAN.

1 Shred any large spinach leaves. Rinse the spinach under cold water, then put in a large pan with just the rinsing water clinging to the leaves. Cover and cook for about 1 minute or until the leaves have wilted. Remove from the pan and leave to cool.

2 Meanwhile, put the tofu and salmon cubes in a shallow dish. Mix together the rice vinegar, soy sauce, garlic, and mustard powder, and pour over the tofu and salmon. Cover and leave to marinate for 1 hour or longer. Preheat the oven to 375°F.

3 Brush the base and sides of a fairly deep 9-inch flan dish with a little sunflower oil. Unwrap the phyllo sheets and line the dish with five sheets, brushing each one with a little oil and leaving any excess to overhang the sides of the dish.

4 Spread the spinach over the pastry base. Drain the tofu and salmon from the marinade and spoon over the spinach. Crumple the pastry edges over the top, filling in gaps with the remaining sheets.

5 Brush the top of the pie with a little more oil and sprinkle over the sesame seeds. Stand the dish on a cookie sheet and bake for 45 to 50 minutes or until golden brown.

6 Serve hot with cheese sauce, low-calorie lemon mayonnaise or plain with a tomato, onion, and basil salad.

nutrition facts	
energy	250 cal
	1027 kJ
protein	18 g
fat	15 g
of which saturated	2 g
carbohydrate	11 g
fiber	2 g
cholesterol	29 mg
sodium	427 mg

teriyaki **shrimp** with tofu

SERVES 4

6 Tbsp sunflower oil

1 lb raw shrimp, peeled

9 oz firm tofu, cubed

2 Tbsp light soy sauce

2 Tbsp bottled teriyaki marinade

1 Tbsp lime juice

2 Tbsp rice vinegar

2 tsp honey

1 tsp sesame oil

1 red bell pepper, seeded and
    sliced thin

6 scallions, sliced

8-oz can water chestnuts,
    drained and sliced

1½ cups thin egg noodles

⅔ cup bean sprouts

2 Tbsp shredded scallions

THESE SWEET-AND-SOUR SHRIMP WITH TOFU MAKE A DELICIOUSLY LIGHT SUMMER LUNCH OR SUPPER DISH. THE QUANTITIES CAN EASILY BE DOUBLED AND SERVED AS PART OF A BUFFET SPREAD.

1 Heat 2 tablespoons of the sunflower oil in a large skillet and sauté the shrimp and tofu in two batches for 5 minutes until the shrimp turn opaque and the tofu is golden. Transfer to a bowl.

2 Mix together the soy sauce, teriyaki marinade, lime juice, vinegar, honey, sesame oil, and remaining sunflower oil, and pour over the shrimp and tofu. Stir to mix, leave to cool, cover, and set aside in a cool place for 1 to 2 hours.

3 Drain the shrimp and tofu (reserve the marinade) and mix with the bell pepper, scallions, and water chestnuts.

4 Cook the noodles in a pan of boiling water for 5 minutes or according to the instructions on the package. Drain and, while still hot, toss with the bean sprouts and reserved marinade. Transfer to a serving bowl and spoon the tofu mixture on top. Scatter over the scallions and chill until ready to serve.

nutrition facts	
energy	525 cal
	2195 kJ
protein	34 g
fat	24 g
of which saturated	4 g
carbohydrate	45 g
fiber	3 g
cholesterol	233 mg
sodium	1165 mg

sweet-and-sour **prawns** with tofu and mango

SERVES 4

2 Tbsp sunflower oil

1 medium onion, peeled and
    finely chopped

1 medium carrot, peeled and
    grated

1 tsp fresh garlic purée

2 tsp red curry paste

14-oz can plum tomatoes

Juice of 1 lime

2 Tbsp light soy sauce

2 Tbsp tomato paste

1 Tbsp brown sugar

1 lb green tiger prawns, peeled

9 oz firm tofu, cubed

1 small mango, peeled and flesh
    chopped

GREEN TIGER PRAWNS ARE BEST FOR THIS DISH AS THEY WILL ABSORB THE SPICINESS OF THE SWEET-AND-SOUR SAUCE, SO WILL HAVE A BETTER FLAVOR AND TEXTURE THAN PRECOOKED ONES.

1 Heat the oil in a large pan and add the onion, carrot, and garlic. Sauté for 5 minutes, then stir in the curry paste, tomatoes and their juice, lime juice, soy sauce, tomato paste, and brown sugar. Cover the pan and simmer over a low heat for 30 minutes.

2 Purée in a food processor or push through a coarse sieve. Return the sauce to the pan, stir in the prawns, tofu, and mango, and cook gently for 5 minutes or until the prawns turn pink. Serve at once with mixed long-grain and wild rice.

nutrition facts	
energy	290 cal
	1210 kJ
protein	28 g
fat	10 g
of which saturated	1 g
carbohydrate	23 g
fiber	4 g
cholesterol	219 mg
sodium	749 mg

spice-crusted **tuna** with vegetables and tofu

SERVES 4

4 tuna steaks

2 Tbsp coriander seeds,
   finely crushed

1 tsp chili sauce

2 tsp fresh ginger purée

1¼ cups French beans, trimmed

½ bunch of asparagus spears

1 bunch of scallions, trimmed

3 Tbsp vegetable or peanut oil

2 Tbsp butter

9 oz firm tofu, cut into sticks
   measuring roughly 2 in x ½ in

Juice of 2 limes

Small bunch of fresh cilantro,
   and 4 Tbsp chopped fresh
   parsley, to garnish

COOKING TIME FOR THE TUNA WILL DEPEND ON HOW THICK THE
STEAKS ARE AND HOW RARE YOU LIKE YOUR FISH—ALLOW
BETWEEN 1 TO 2 MINUTES A SIDE OVER A FAIRLY BRISK HEAT.

1 Place the tuna steaks side by side in a shallow dish. Mix together the crushed coriander, chili, and ginger, and spread over the fish. Leave to stand in a cool place for 1 hour. Steam the French beans, asparagus, and scallions for 5 minutes or until just tender. Keep warm in a low oven.

2 Heat a ridged grill pan until very hot, then add the oil and butter. When foaming, add the tuna steaks, spiced sides down, with any juices from the dish. Sauté for 1 to 2 minutes, turn over, and continue to cook for 1 to 2 minutes or until done to your liking. Drain from the pan and keep warm with the vegetables.

3 Add the tofu and sauté for 2 to 3 minutes until heated through, then squeeze in the lime juice. Arrange the vegetables and tofu on serving plates with the tuna steaks on top. Stir the pan juices briefly and spoon over the steaks. Tuck a few cilantro leaves among the vegetables and tofu, and scatter the parsley over the tuna.

nutrition facts	
energy	443 cal
	1850 kJ
protein	49 g
fat	25 g
of which saturated	7 g
carbohydrate	6 g
fiber	3 g
cholesterol	63 mg
sodium	173 mg

crisp-topped white **fish**, broccoli, and tofu

SERVES 4

1½ cups broccoli florets

1 Tbsp sunflower oil

2¼ cups button mushrooms, cut
   into halves

1½ cups store-bought arrabiata
   or tomato pasta sauce

9 oz firm tofu, cubed

11 oz white fish fillet, skinned
   and cut into chunks

FOR THE TOPPING:

⅔ cup fresh whole-wheat
   breadcrumbs

½ cup bran flakes or cornflakes,
   crushed

1 Tbsp chopped hazelnuts

2 Tbsp chopped fresh parsley

½ cup grated Cheddar cheese

ANY WHITE FISH CAN BE USED FOR THIS RECIPE—COD, HADDOCK,
FLOUNDER, OR ANGLER FISH WOULD ALL BE SUITABLE.

1 Cook the broccoli in a pan of boiling water for 3 minutes and then drain.

2 Heat the oil in a large pan and sauté the mushrooms for 5 minutes. Stir in the pasta sauce, tofu, fish, and broccoli, and bring to a boil. Lower the heat and cook gently for 5 minutes or until the fish is opaque. Spoon the mixture into a shallow heatproof dish and preheat the broiler.

3 For the topping, mix together the breadcrumbs, crushed bran flakes or cornflakes, hazelnuts, parsley, and cheese. Sprinkle over the fish mixture in an even layer and broil until the topping browns. Alternatively, make the dish ahead and when ready to serve, reheat in a 375°F oven for 25 to 30 minutes until piping hot throughout.

nutrition facts	
energy	310 cal
	1205 kJ
protein	29 g
fat	14 g
of which saturated	4 g
carbohydrate	16 g
fiber	3 g
cholesterol	47 mg
sodium	587 mg

tofu, tuna, and **zucchini** cheese bake

SERVES 4

2 Tbsp sunflower oil

9 oz fresh tuna, cut into
2½- x 1-in strips

2 cups cauliflower florets

1 large carrot, sliced

1 large zucchini, cut into small
chunks

9 oz firm tofu, cut into
1-in cubes

⅓ cup all-purpose flour

1 tsp mustard powder

2 cups low-fat milk

⅔ cup grated aged Cheddar
cheese

¼ cup grated red Leicester
cheese

2 Tbsp dry breadcrumbs

½ tsp paprika

Green salad, to serve

A USEFUL RECIPE IF YOU HAVE LEFTOVER COOKED VEGETABLES THAT
NEED USING UP. CHOP THEM INTO BITE-SIZE PIECES AND MIX WITH
THE COOKED TUNA AND TOFU.

1 Heat the oil in a skillet until hot, and sear the tuna over a brisk heat for 2 minutes on each side until browned.

2 Meanwhile, cook the cauliflower and carrot slices in a saucepan of boiling water until just tender.

3 Drain the tuna from the skillet, add the zucchini chunks and tofu, lower the heat, and sauté for 5 minutes. Remove from the pan, mix with the tuna, cauliflower, and carrot, and spoon into an ovenproof dish.

3 Preheat the oven to 350°F.

4 Whisk the flour and mustard powder with a little of the milk until smooth. Add to the skillet with the rest of the milk, and stir over a medium heat until thickened and smooth. Stir in 2 ounces of the Cheddar and spoon over the tuna and tofu mixture. Sprinkle over the remaining Cheddar, red Leicester cheese, breadcrumbs, and paprika, and bake for 25 to 30 minutes until golden and bubbling. Serve with a green salad.

nutrition facts	
energy	440 cal
	1846 kJ
protein	35 g
fat	22 g
of which saturated	8.5 g
carbohydrate	26 g
fiber	3 g
cholesterol	50 mg
sodium	337 mg

nasi **goreng**

SERVES 4

2 eggs

Salt and pepper

3 Tbsp vegetable oil

8 scallions, sliced thin

1 red bell pepper, seeded and
sliced thin

½ cup sugar snap peas, cut into
halves

8 oz lean pork steak, cut into
thin strips

9 oz firm tofu cut into batons

6 oz green prawns, peeled

2 cups cold, cooked long-grain
rice

2 Tbsp sweet soy sauce

½ tsp dried shrimp paste

1 tsp sambal oelek

"NASI" IS RICE AND "GORENG" MEANS FRIED IN INDONESIA, WHERE
THIS STIR-FRY COMBINATION TOPPED WITH SHREDDED OMELET IS A
NATIONAL DISH. SAMBAL OELEK IS A HOT CHOPPED CHILI CONDIMENT
THAT CAN BE FOUND IN SUPERMARKETS AND ASIAN FOOD STORES.

1 Beat the eggs with seasoning and 1 tablespoon of water. Heat 1 tablespoon of the oil in a wok or large skillet, add the eggs, and cook for 2 to 3 minutes to make a thin, unfolded omelet. Slice out of the pan onto a board and set aside.

2 Add another tablespoon of the oil to the pan and stir-fry the scallions, bell pepper, and sugar snap peas for 5 minutes. Remove from the pan. Add the remaining oil to the pan, turn up the heat to fairly high and stir-fry the pork and tofu for 5 minutes until browned.

3 Lower the heat to medium, return the vegetables to the pan, and add the prawns, rice, soy sauce, shrimp paste, and sambal oelek. Toss over the heat for about 5 minutes or until the prawns turn pink and everything is piping hot.

4 Roll the omelet and cut into thin slices. Serve the fried rice with the omelet strips scattered over the top.

nutrition facts	
energy	440 cal
	1830 kJ
protein	33 g
fat	20 g
of which saturated	4 g
carbohydrate	33 g
fiber	2 g
cholesterol	245 mg
sodium	632 mg

seafood and tofu casserole with tapenade croûtes

SERVES 6

2 Tbsp olive oil

2 medium onions, peeled and sliced

2 garlic cloves, peeled and chopped

1 medium carrot, sliced

1 green bell pepper, seeded and chopped

9 oz firm tofu, cut into bite-size pieces

14-oz can chopped tomatoes with herbs

1½ cups fish broth

¾ cup dry white wine

2 bay leaves

2 tsp chopped fresh oregano leaves

1 lb anglerfish fillet, cut into bite-size pieces

6 oz green tiger prawns, peeled

1 Tbsp lemon juice

Salt and pepper

FOR THE CROÛTES:

12 slices of French bread

Small jar of tapenade

TAPENADE IS A PUNGENT PROVENÇAL BLEND OF SMALL BLACK NIÇOISE OLIVES, ANCHOVIES, OLIVE OIL, AND CAPERS—TAPENA BEING THE PROVENÇAL WORD FOR CAPERS. YOU CAN BUY IT READY-MADE FROM DELICATESSENS AND SPECIALTY FOOD STORES.

1 Heat the oil in a large saucepan or flameproof casserole, add the onions, garlic, carrot, bell pepper, and tofu, and sauté over a low heat for 10 minutes.

2 Add the tomatoes, broth, wine, bay leaves, and oregano, and bring to a simmer. Cook for 10 minutes or until the carrot slices are tender. Add the anglerfish, prawns, and lemon juice, and season with salt and pepper. Simmer for about 5 minutes or until the anglerfish is cooked and the prawns are pink.

3 For the croûtes, toast the bread slices and spread with the tapenade. Keep warm in a low oven until the seafood mixture is ready.

4 Ladle the mixture into serving bowls, and serve the tapenade croûtes separately.

nutrition facts	
energy	400 cal
	1643 kJ
protein	28 g
fat	11 g
of which saturated	2 g
carbohydrate	43 g
fiber	4 g
cholesterol	67 mg
sodium	1216 mg

laksa

SERVES 4

3 Tbsp peanut oil

2 onions, peeled and finely sliced

2 garlic cloves, peeled and chopped

2 Tbsp ground almonds

1 Tbsp ground coriander

1 tsp cumin

1 tsp turmeric

2 red chiles

1 tsp fish sauce

2 Tbsp red curry paste

5 cups coconut milk

1 Tbsp brown sugar

Salt and pepper

9 oz firm tofu, cut into cubes

2 chicken breasts, sliced

¾ cup bean sprouts

2 Tbsp chopped fresh cilantro

1 cup dried rice noodles

A POPULAR DISH IN MALAYSIA. ITS NAME TRANSLATES AS A SOUP BUT IT IS REALLY A MEAL IN ITSELF.

1 Heat 1 tablespoon oil in a wok or deep skillet and sauté the onions and garlic over a low heat for 10 minutes until soft.

2 Sprinkle in the ground almonds, coriander, cumin, and turmeric. Deseed and finely chop one chile and add to the pan with the fish sauce and curry paste. Stir and cook gently for 5 minutes. Stir in the coconut milk and sugar, and season to taste. Bring to a simmer and cook for 5 minutes.

3 Meanwhile, heat the remaining oil in another pan and sauté the tofu in two batches for 5 minutes until golden on all sides. Drain and keep warm. Add the chicken to the pan and stir-fry for 5 minutes, add the bean sprouts and cilantro and cook for another 2 minutes. Break up the noodles and place in a bowl. Pour over boiling water to cover and leave to stand for 3 to 4 minutes until softened. Drain well.

4 To serve, divide the noodles, tofu, and chicken mixture among four soup bowls and ladle over the coconut sauce. Sprinkle with the chopped cilantro and the remaining chile, finely sliced.

nutrition facts	
energy	1000 cal
	4422 kJ
protein	30 g
fat	73 g
of which saturated	44 g
carbohydrate	46 g
fiber	3 g
cholesterol	62 mg
sodium	206 mg

chicken and tofu masala

SERVES 4

1 Tbsp vegetable oil

2 boneless chicken breasts, skinned and cubed

9 oz firm tofu, cubed

1 large onion, peeled and sliced

2 Tbsp masala curry paste

1 tsp chili powder

1½ cups chicken broth

8-oz can chopped tomatoes

1 green bell pepper, seeded and sliced

1 cup baby corn

8-10 new potatoes, cut into halves

2 tsp cornstarch

½ cup plain yogurt

SERVE THIS CREAMED CURRY WITH TRADITIONAL ACCOMPANIMENTS SUCH AS PAPPADAMS OR POORI, MANGO CHUTNEY, AND A COOLING SAMBAL OF FINELY CHOPPED TOMATOES AND RED ONION.

1 Heat the oil in a large pan and fry the chicken and tofu in batches over a fairly high heat until lightly browned. Remove from the pan and set aside.

2 Add the onion, lower the heat, and sauté until soft. Stir in the curry paste and chili powder and cook for 2 minutes. Add the broth and tomatoes, and bring to a simmer. Lower the heat, return the chicken and tofu to the pan, and add the bell pepper, corn, and potatoes. Cover and cook for 30 minutes or until the potatoes are tender.

3 Mix the cornstarch into the yogurt and stir into the pan. Simmer for 5 more minutes. Serve with boiled or pilaf rice and curry accompaniments.

nutrition facts	
energy	300 cal
	1261 kJ
protein	27 g
fat	12 g
of which saturated	2.5 g
carbohydrate	23 g
fiber	3 g
cholesterol	47 mg
sodium	705 mg

thai green **chicken** and tofu curry

SERVES 4

2 Tbsp peanut oil

1 red onion, peeled and chopped

1 large potato, peeled and cut into small chunks

1 medium eggplant, cut into small chunks

1 green bell pepper, seeded and chopped

2 boneless chicken breasts, skinned and cut into chunks

9 oz firm tofu, cubed

2 Tbsp green curry paste

1 tsp tamarind purée

1 tsp fresh ginger purée

3 Tbsp whole-nut crunchy peanut butter

1½ cups chicken broth

2 tsp brown sugar

2 Tbsp dark soy sauce

ACCOMPANY THIS SWEET-AND-SOUR CURRY WITH THAI FRAGRANT RICE AND A SIDE DISH OF SMALL PIECES OF FRESH PINEAPPLE SPRINKLED WITH CHOPPED LEAF CILANTRO.

1 Heat the oil in a large pan, add the onion and potato chunks, and sauté for 5 minutes, stirring occasionally. Add the eggplant and pepper, stir well, and sauté for 5 minutes more.
2 Add the chicken and cook until the flesh becomes light-colored, then add the tofu. Stir in the curry paste, tamarind, and ginger and cook for 2 to 3 minutes.
3 Add the peanut butter, broth, sugar, and soy sauce, and stir until simmering. Cover the pan, lower the heat, and cook gently for 15 minutes. Serve with rice.

nutrition facts	
energy	400 cal
	1690 kJ
protein	29 g
fat	19 g
of which saturated	3 g
carbohydrate	21 g
fiber	5 g
cholesterol	32 mg
sodium	831 mg

lemon-and-**ginger** chicken with tofu

SERVES 4

8 shallots

2 Tbsp sunflower oil

8 chicken thighs, skinned

2 bacon slices, chopped

4 oz firm tofu, cut into small cubes

1¾ cups mushrooms, sliced

¾ cup chicken broth

Juice and finely grated rind of 1 large lemon

1 tsp fresh ginger purée

1 Tbsp sun-dried tomato paste

4 Tbsp low-fat soured cream

Salt and pepper

STIR THE LOW-FAT SOURED CREAM INTO THE SAUCE A LITTLE AT A TIME AND DO NOT LET IT BOIL OR IT WILL SEPARATE. A TEASPOON OF CORNSTARCH STIRRED INTO THE SOURED CREAM WILL STABILIZE IT.

1 Put the shallots in a saucepan, cover with cold water, and bring to a boil. Cook for 1 minute, then drain, and cool under cold water. Pull off the skins and halve each shallot.
2 Heat the oil in a large skillet and brown the chicken thighs on both sides. Remove from the pan and set aside. Add the chopped bacon, shallots, and tofu, and fry over a gentle heat for about 5 minutes, stirring occasionally, until softened and starting to brown. Add the mushrooms and cook for another couple of minutes, then add the broth, lemon juice and rind, ginger purée, and tomato paste. Return the chicken to the pan, cover, and simmer for 15 minutes or until cooked through.
3 Stir the soured cream gradually into the sauce and season with salt and pepper. Serve with rice or pasta and a green vegetable.

nutrition facts	
energy	330 cal
	1372 kJ
protein	38 g
fat	17 g
of which saturated	5 g
carbohydrate	6 g
fiber	1 g
cholesterol	88 mg
sodium	470 mg

chicken, **bok choy,** and tofu stir-fry

SERVES 4

9 oz firm tofu, cut into small cubes

2 boneless chicken breasts, skinned and cut into bite-size pieces

3 Tbsp hot mango chutney

Juice of 1 lime

3 Tbsp teriyaki marinade

3 Tbsp peanut oil

¾ cup cashew nuts

1 carrot, cut into thin matchsticks

4 scallions, sliced (keep the tops for garnish)

2 heads of bok choy, shredded and stalks removed

WHEN STIR-FRYING THE CASHEWS, REMOVE FROM THE PAN WHEN LIGHTLY GOLDEN OR THEY WILL QUICKLY BURN AND BECOME BITTER.

1 Put the tofu and chicken in a shallow dish. Mix together the mango chutney (remove any large pieces of fruit), lime juice, teriyaki marinade, and 1 tablespoon of oil. Spoon over the tofu and chicken and turn the pieces until coated. Cover and set aside for 1 hour to cool.

2 Heat 1 tablespoon of oil in a wok or large skillet, add the cashews, and toss them over the heat for about 30 seconds until golden. Remove from the pan and drain on paper towels. Add the carrot and stir-fry for 5 minutes, then add the scallions and bok choy. Stir-fry for 5 more minutes, then remove from the pan and set aside. Drain the tofu and chicken and add to the pan with the remaining oil. Stir-fry over a brisk heat for 3 to 4 minutes. Return the vegetables to the pan and pour over any remaining marinade.

3 Toss together for 2 to 3 minutes to heat through, add the cashews, and serve at once,

nutrition facts	
energy	330 cal
	1379 kJ
protein	26 g
fat	19 g
of which saturated	3 g
carbohydrate	13 g
fiber	2 g
cholesterol	32 mg
sodium	872 mg

vietnamese **chicken** and tofu curry

SERVES 4

1 onion, peeled and chopped

2 garlic cloves, peeled and chopped

Small piece of fresh ginger, peeled and chopped

1 fresh lemon grass sprig, chopped

2 Tbsp vegetable oil

2 medium sweet potatoes, peeled and cut into 1-in chunks

1 Tbsp madras curry paste

1 tsp ground turmeric

1 tsp chili powder

9 oz chicken breasts, skinned and cut into bite-size pieces

9 oz firm tofu, cubed

1½ cups chicken broth

¾ cup coconut milk

Salt and pepper

3 Tbsp chopped flat-leaf parsley

VIETNAMESE CUISINE BLENDS ASIAN SPICES AND SAUCES WITH THE MORE WESTERN FLAVORS OF EUROPEAN HERBS AND VEGETABLES, A LEGACY FROM ITS FRENCH COLONIAL PAST. SWEET POTATOES ADD AN ATTRACTIVE SWEETNESS TO THIS CREAMY CURRY.

1 Place the onion, garlic, ginger, and lemon grass in a food processor and blend to a smooth paste.

2 Heat the oil in a large pan, add the sweet potato, and sauté over a low heat for 5 minutes. Add the onion paste and cook for another 5 minutes, stirring occasionally, then add the curry paste, turmeric, and chili powder.

3 Add the chicken and tofu, and stir to coat with the spices. Pour in the broth and bring to a boil. Simmer gently for 15 minutes, then add the coconut milk, and simmer for 15 more minutes or until the sweet potato and chicken are cooked. Season and serve the curry garnished with chopped parsley. Accompany with boiled rice.

nutrition facts	
energy	380 cal
	1606 kJ
protein	20 g
fat	22 g
of which saturated	10 g
carbohydrate	22 g
fiber	2.5 g
cholesterol	36 mg
sodium	327 mg

RIGHT chicken, bok choy, and tofu stir-fry

duck, toulouse sausage, and tofu cassoulet

SERVES 4

9 oz firm tofu, cubed

1 tsp paprika

8-oz can chopped tomatoes

1 large duck breast

8 Toulouse sausages

1 large red onion, peeled and sliced

2 large carrots, sliced thin

1½ cups cauliflower florets

2½ cups button mushrooms, cut into halves

1½ cups vegetable broth

2 Tbsp tomato paste

Two 15-oz cans cannellini beans, drained and rinsed

Salt and pepper

1⅔ cups fresh breadcrumbs

2 Tbsp chopped fresh parsley

½ cup grated Gruyère cheese

IF YOU REMOVE THE SKIN FROM THE DUCK BREAST, ADD A TABLESPOON OF OIL TO THE PAN WHEN FRYING IT WITH THE SAUSAGES.

1 Put the tofu cubes in a bowl and add the paprika and tomatoes. Set aside for 30 minutes.

2 Dry-fry the duck breast and sausages in a heavy skillet until well browned on all sides. Drain and cut the duck and sausages into chunks.

3 Add 2 tablespoons fat from the pan to a large saucepan or flameproof casserole and when hot, fry the onion and carrots for 5 minutes. Add the cauliflower and mushrooms, and fry for 5 more minutes, then stir in the tofu and tomatoes, broth, tomato paste, and beans. Bring to a boil, season to taste, and add the sausages and duck. Cover and simmer gently for 30 to 40 minutes until the carrots and cauliflower are tender.

4 Preheat the broiler. Spoon the cassoulet into a heatproof dish. Mix the breadcrumbs, parsley, and cheese together, and sprinkle over the top. Broil until browned.

nutrition facts	
energy	700 cal
	2948 kJ
protein	44 g
fat	28 g
of which saturated	10 g
carbohydrate	73 g
fiber	17 g
cholesterol	83 mg
sodium	1801 mg

pork and tofu in **black bean** sauce

SERVES 4

9 oz firm tofu, cut into batons

12 oz lean pork steaks, cut into strips

1 pineapple ring, cut into chunks

1 tsp sesame oil

2 Tbsp sweet soy sauce

1 tsp fresh garlic purée

1 Tbsp honey

2 Tbsp peanut oil

1 red bell pepper, seeded and sliced

8 baby corn, halved lengthwise

1 celery rib, sliced

1½ cups button mushrooms, halved

5½-oz jar black bean stir-fry sauce

CRISPY SEAWEED MAKES A GOOD ACCOMPANIMENT TO THIS DISH. IF YOU MAKE YOUR OWN, TAKE CARE WHEN DEEP-FRYING THE SPRING GREENS—THEY WILL SPIT.

1 Put the tofu, pork, and pineapple chunks in a shallow dish. Mix together the sesame oil, soy sauce, garlic, honey, and any juice that runs out of the pineapple, and add, turning over until the pieces are coated. Cover and set aside in a cool place for 1 hour.

2 Heat half the peanut oil in a wok or large skillet, add the bell pepper, corn, celery, and mushrooms, and stir-fry for 5 minutes or until starting to soften. Remove from the pan and set aside.

3 Add the rest of the oil to the pan, drain the tofu, pork, and pineapple from the marinade and put into the pan. Stir-fry over a high heat for 5 minutes. Add the black bean sauce, return the vegetables to the pan, and pour in any marinade left in the dish. Toss together for 2 to 3 minutes until piping hot. Serve immediately.

nutrition facts	
energy	315 cal
	1316 kJ
protein	28 g
fat	16 g
of which saturated	3.5 g
carbohydrate	14 g
fiber	2.5 g
cholesterol	60 mg
sodium	1463 mg

marinated **duck** and tofu salad

SERVES 4

3 shallots, peeled and chopped

3 garlic cloves, peeled and finely chopped

1 green chile, seeded and finely chopped

1 tsp fresh ginger purée

2 tsp sesame oil

2 duck breasts

9 oz firm tofu, cut into batons

1½ cups water chestnuts, sliced

½ cucumber, cut into batons

1 green bell pepper, seeded and sliced

¾ cup bok choy, shredded

FOR THE DRESSING:

1 tsp fresh lemon grass purée

3 Tbsp peanut oil

2 Tbsp light soy sauce

1 Tbsp lime juice

1 tsp liquid honey

THIS UNUSUAL SALAD CAN BE SERVED AS A LUNCH DISH OR AS PART OF A BUFFET SPREAD. WHEN YOU COOK THE DUCK BREASTS, SAUTÉ THEM WITH THE SKIN ON IN A HEAVY PAN OVER A HIGH HEAT UNTIL DONE TO YOUR LIKING.

1 For the marinade, blend the shallots, garlic, chile, ginger, and sesame oil together in a food processor to make a thick paste. Slash the duck skin with a sharp knife at ½-inch intervals, place in a shallow dish with the tofu, and spread with the marinade. Cover and chill for 2 to 3 hours.

2 Heat a heavy, nonstick skillet or ridged broiler pan until very hot. Lift the duck breasts from the dish, add to the pan, and cook for 5 to 6 minutes on each side. Remove from the pan, add the tofu, and cook for a couple of minutes until the batons are golden. Remove the tofu and set aside.

3 Pull the skin off the duck breasts and slice the flesh thinly on a slant. Mix with the tofu, water chestnuts, cucumber, bell pepper, and bok choy, and spoon into a serving dish.

4 Whisk the dressing ingredients together, strain in any marinade left in the dish, and pour over the salad. Cover and chill for 1 hour or until ready to serve.

nutrition facts	
energy	290 cal
	1219 kJ
protein	25 g
fat	17 g
of which saturated	3 g
carbohydrate	10 g
fiber	2 g
cholesterol	96 mg
sodium	539 mg

sausage, carrot, and tofu hotchpotch

SERVES 4

8 large sausages

2 Tbsp sunflower oil

1 onion, peeled and sliced thin

9 oz firm tofu, cut into batons

1½ cups carrots, sliced

1 tsp paprika

2¾ cups vegetable broth

2 Tbsp tomato paste

1 Tbsp Worcestershire sauce

15-oz can cannellini beans, drained and rinsed

1¼ cups frozen fava beans

2 tsp chopped fresh thyme leaves

Freshly ground black pepper

2 large potatoes, peeled and sliced thin

BUY THE HIGHEST QUALITY BREAKFAST LINKS FOR THIS RECIPE AS THEY WILL HAVE A HIGHER PERCENTAGE OF LEAN MEAT. EUROPEAN-STYLE SAUSAGES, SUCH AS TOULOUSE, WOULD ALSO WORK WELL IN THIS DISH.

1 Preheat the oven to 325°F. Sauté the sausages in 1 tablespoon of the oil until browned all over. Remove from the pan and place in a casserole. If the sausages have produced a lot of fat, drain off all but 1 tablespoonful.

2 Add the onion, tofu, and carrots to the pan, and sauté for 5 minutes. Sprinkle over the paprika and cook for another 5 minutes, then pour in the broth and add the tomato paste, Worcestershire sauce, cannellini beans, fava beans, and thyme. Bring to a boil and season with pepper.

3 Pour into the casserole and arrange the potato slices on top. Cover and cook in the oven for 45 minutes.

4 Increase the oven temperature to 400°F. Remove the lid from the casserole, brush the potato slices with the remaining oil, and return to the oven uncovered for 20 minutes, or until the potato slices are browned and tender.

nutrition facts	
energy	676 cal
	2823 kJ
protein	29 g
fat	37 g
of which saturated	12.5 g
carbohydrate	60 g
fiber	12 g
cholesterol	45mg
sodium	1727 mg

ham braised with tofu and **leeks**

SERVES 4

1½ lb piece of ham

2 Tbsp sunflower oil

1½ cups small carrots

2 large rutabaga or turnips, peeled and cut into small chunks

9 oz firm tofu, cubed

1¾ cups dry cider

2¾ cups chicken broth

2 Tbsp all-purpose flour

Freshly ground black pepper

4-6 small potatoes, scrubbed or peeled if preferred

2 leeks, cut into ½-in slices

BUY A SMALL PIECE OF HAM FOR THIS RECIPE AND CUT IT INTO CHUNKS. SMOKED OR UNSMOKED HAM IS SUITABLE AND NEITHER REQUIRES SOAKING BEFORE COOKING.

1 Trim the fat from the ham and cut the meat into 1½-inch chunks. Heat the oil in a skillet and lightly brown the ham in batches. Transfer to a large saucepan or casserole.

2 Add the carrots, rutabaga or turnips, and tofu to the pan and sauté for 5 minutes. Transfer to the saucepan or casserole.

3 Pour the cider into the pan. Mix a little of the broth with the flour and add to the pan with the rest of the broth. Season with freshly ground black pepper and bring to a boil.

4 Pour over the ham, tofu, and vegetables, and either cover and simmer over a gentle heat for 30 minutes or cook in a 325°F oven. Add the potatoes and leeks, and cook for 45 minutes more or until the ham and vegetables are tender.

nutrition facts	
energy	510 cal
	2134 kJ
protein	42 g
fat	21 g
of which saturated	6 g
carbohydrate	30 g
fiber	4.5 g
cholesterol	30 mg
sodium	3389 mg

ranchero pie with rosti

SERVES 4

3 Tbsp sunflower oil

1 large onion, peeled and chopped

9 oz lean ground lamb

9 oz firm tofu, frozen, defrosted, and grated

1¾ cups mushrooms, sliced

14-oz can chopped tomatoes with herbs

2 Tbsp tomato paste

¼ cup red wine

1½ cups chicken broth

15-oz can mixed beans in spiced tomato sauce

Salt and pepper

2 lb mixed root vegetables, such as potatoes, carrots, parsnips

MIXING CHOPPED TOFU HALF-AND-HALF WITH RED MEAT LOWERS THE SATURATED FAT IN A RECIPE BY 50 PERCENT. IF YOU WANT TO REDUCE THE FAT EVEN MORE, USE CHOPPED TURKEY OR CHICKEN IN THIS RECIPE INSTEAD OF THE LAMB.

1 Heat 1 tablespoon of the oil in a large pan and cook the onion until soft. Add the ground lamb, sauté until browned, then stir in the tofu and mushrooms. Cook for 5 minutes, add the tomatoes, tomato paste, red wine, and broth. Bring to a simmer and leave to bubble steadily for about 30 minutes until reduced and thickened. Stir in the beans and their sauce, and season to taste.

2 Peel the vegetables and cook in a pan of boiling water until just tender. Drain, cool, and coarsely grate. Mix with the remaining oil and season to taste.

3 Preheat the oven to 400°F. Spoon the lamb mixture into an ovenproof dish and spread the vegetable mixture over the top. Bake in the oven for 25 to 30 minutes or until the topping is crisp and golden.

nutrition facts	
energy	530 cal
	2223 kJ
protein	31 g
fat	18 g
of which saturated	4 g
carbohydrate	63 g
fiber	9 g
cholesterol	49 mg
sodium	875 mg

spiced sesame **lamb** and tofu

SERVES 4

2 cups thread egg noodles

1½ cups small broccoli florets

2 Tbsp peanut oil

1 orange bell pepper, seeded and chopped

8 cherry tomatoes, cut into halves

2 Tbsp light soy sauce

12 oz lean lamb, cut into strips

9 oz firm tofu, cubed

4 Tbsp hoisin sauce

2 tsp Thai red curry paste

2 Tbsp sesame seeds

TRIM ANY FAT FROM THE LAMB BEFORE SLICING INTO STRIPS. LEAN MEAT CUT FROM THE LEG OR FILLET IS THE MOST TENDER AND IDEAL FOR A QUICK-COOK DISH LIKE THIS. MAKE SURE THE PAN IS VERY HOT BEFORE ADDING THE LAMB AND TOFU SO THAT THE LAMB SEALS IMMEDIATELY AND DOES NOT TOUGHEN.

1 Bring a pan of water to a boil and add the noodles. Place a steamer on top and put the broccoli in this. Cook for 4 minutes or until both are tender, then remove the broccoli from the steamer and drain the noodles.

2 Meanwhile, heat 1 tablespoon of the oil in a wok or large skillet and stir-fry the pepper for 5 minutes until starting to soften. Add the cherry tomatoes and broccoli, and stir-fry for 2 more minutes, then tip in the noodles. Add the soy sauce and toss well together. Transfer to a serving bowl and keep warm in a low oven.

3 Pour the remaining oil into the pan, turn up the heat to medium-high, and add the lamb and tofu. Stir-fry for 5 minutes, add the hoisin sauce and curry paste, and toss together until the meat and tofu are coated. Sprinkle with the sesame seeds, spoon over the noodles and vegetables, and serve.

nutrition facts	
energy	577 cal
	2423 kJ
protein	36 g
fat	26 g
of which saturated	7 g
carbohydrate	52 g
fiber	5 g
cholesterol	88 mg
sodium	1293 mg

steak with **blue cheese** and tofu sauce

SERVES 4

4 sirloin or rump steaks

FOR THE SAUCE:

9 oz firm tofu

½ cup Roquefort cheese

1 cup milk

2 tsp chopped fresh thyme leaves

1 tsp Dijon mustard

Thyme, to garnish

CHOPPED TOMATOES AND STEAMED BROCCOLI MAKE COLORFUL ACCOMPANIMENTS TO THE STEAK. THE SAUCE COULD ALSO BE SERVED WITH GRILLED PORK STEAKS, POTATOES BAKED IN THEIR SKINS, OR ROAST CHICKEN. ANY MEAT JUICES FROM THE BROILER PAN CAN BE STIRRED INTO THE SAUCE AT THE END, IF YOU LIKE.

1 Grill the steaks for about 3 minutes on each side, or until done to your liking.

2 Meanwhile, make the sauce. Purée the tofu, cheese, milk, thyme, and mustard together in a food processor, or mash the tofu and cheese in a bowl and stir in the other ingredients. Transfer to a saucepan and heat gently until simmering. Keep over a low heat, without letting the sauce boil, until the steaks are ready.

3 Serve the sauce spooned over the steaks and garnish with thyme.

nutrition facts	
energy	364 cal
	1523 kJ
protein	46 g
fat	19 g
of which saturated	9 g
carbohydrate	3 g
fiber	0 g
cholesterol	127 mg
sodium	450 mg

ground **steak** and tofu thatch

SERVES 4

1 Tbsp sunflower oil

1 red onion, peeled and sliced thin

1 lb lean ground steak

9 oz firm tofu, frozen, defrosted, and grated or finely chopped

2 medium carrots, finely diced

2¼ cups baby button mushrooms

2 cups beef broth

2 Tbsp tomato paste

Salt and pepper

FOR THE TOPPING:

3 large potatoes

2 Tbsp olive oil

1 tsp fresh garlic purée

2 egg yolks

2 Tbsp chopped mixed fresh herbs, parsley, chives, thyme, oregano

COOK A DOUBLE QUANTITY OF THE MEAT MIXTURE AND FREEZE HALF AS A TOPPING FOR POTATOES IN THEIR JACKETS OR PASTA FOR ANOTHER MEAL. IF YOU ARE NOT KEEN ON GARLIC, ADD A SPOONFUL OF CREAMED HORSERADISH TO THE MASH INSTEAD.

1 Heat the sunflower oil in a large skillet, add the onion, and sauté until softened. Add the ground steak and cook over a fairly high heat until browned, breaking up any clumps of meat with a wooden spoon.

2 Lower the heat, stir in the tofu, carrots, and mushrooms, and sauté for 5 minutes, stirring occasionally. Add the broth, tomato paste, and seasoning, lower the heat, and simmer uncovered for about 30 minutes until the broth has reduced and the mixture is thick. Spoon into an ovenproof dish and leave to cool.

3 Preheat the oven to 375°F. Peel the potatoes and cut into even-size pieces. Cook in a pan of boiling water until tender, then drain and mash. Return to the pan over a very gentle heat and add the olive oil and garlic. Mix into the potatoes, then remove from the heat and stir in the egg yolks and mixed herbs.

4 Spoon the mash over the meat mixture, stand the dish on a cookie sheet, and bake for 35 to 40 minutes or until brown and crusty on top.

nutrition facts	
energy	510 cal
	2135 kJ
protein	36 g
fat	25 g
of which saturated	7 g
carbohydrate	35 g
fiber	4 g
cholesterol	165 mg
sodium	341 mg

tofu **meatballs** in a rich tomato sauce

SERVES 4–6

- 9 oz firm tofu, frozen, defrosted, and finely chopped or grated
- 9 oz ground pork
- 6 oz sausage meat
- 2 garlic cloves, peeled and crushed
- Salt and freshly ground black pepper
- 1 tsp ground coriander
- 2 Tbsp sunflower oil
- 1 onion, peeled and sliced thin
- 1 red bell pepper, seeded and finely chopped
- Two 14-oz cans chopped tomatoes
- 2 Tbsp sun-dried tomato paste
- 1 Tbsp chopped fresh marjoram
- Spaghetti, to serve
- Basil or marjoram leaves, and freshly grated Parmesan, to garnish

SERVE THE MEATBALLS WITH SPAGHETTI OR ANOTHER PASTA, TOPPED WITH PLENTY OF FRESHLY GRATED PARMESAN. IF YOU WANT TO MAKE THE DISH SPICIER, ADD A TEASPOON OF CHILI PURÉE TO THE TOMATO SAUCE.

1 Put the tofu, pork, sausage meat, garlic, seasoning, and coriander in a bowl and mix together well. With damp hands, shape into small, even-size balls.

2 Heat the oil in a deep, heavy skillet and cook the meatballs in batches until browned all over. Remove from the pan and drain on paper towels.

3 Discard any excess fat from the pan, leaving about 2 tablespoonfuls. Add the onion and bell pepper, and sauté for 5 minutes until softened. Add the tomatoes, tomato paste, and marjoram, and simmer uncovered for 20 minutes, stirring occasionally.

4 Add the meatballs to the sauce, cover, and simmer for 15 minutes, basting them occasionally with the sauce.

5 Serve with spaghetti, garnished with basil or marjoram leaves and freshly grated Parmesan.

nutrition facts	
energy	273 cal
	1138 kJ
protein	17 g
fat	18 g
of which saturated	5 g
carbohydrate	11 g
fiber	2 g
cholesterol	42 mg
sodium	231 mg

4 side dishes and snacks

Whether you're preparing a light lunch, afternoon snack, or side dish for a formal meal, the choices in this chapter range from satay to salsa to vegetarian puff slice. This is the ideal place to discover how to introduce tofu into your diet in deliciously subtle ways—and how to snack in scrumptious style without taking the unhealthy option every time. Many of these dishes go perfectly with the main dishes recipes in the previous chapter. It's simply a case of experimenting—with guaranteed delicious outcomes every time.

LEFT smoked tofu bruschetta (page 110)

vegetable and tofu korma

SERVES 4

6-8 new potatoes, halved

2 medium carrots, sliced

½ medium cauliflower, divided into florets

2 Tbsp sunflower oil

9 oz firm tofu, cubed

1 large onion, peeled and sliced thin

1 yellow zucchini, sliced

3 Tbsp korma curry paste

14-oz can chopped tomatoes

4 Tbsp Greek yogurt

2 garlic cloves, peeled

2 green chiles, halved and seeded

14-oz can garbanzo beans, drained and rinsed

THIS IS AN EXCELLENT SUBSTITUTE FOR A CLASSIC MEAT DISH. SERVE WITH WEDGES OF WARM CORIANDER-AND-GARLIC NAAN BREAD TO SCOOP UP THE DELICIOUS SAUCE.

1 Cook the potatoes and carrots in a saucepan of boiling water for 5 minutes. Add the cauliflower florets and cook for 5 more minutes or until the vegetables are just tender. Drain the vegetables and set aside.

2 Heat the oil in a deep skillet, add the tofu cubes, and cook gently until golden. Drain on paper towels and set aside.

3 Add the onion to the pan and sauté until softened. Add the zucchini and cook for 2 to 3 minutes, then stir in the curry paste, coating the vegetables.

4 Liquidize the tomatoes, yogurt, garlic, and chiles until smooth and add to the pan with the garbanzo beans and tofu. Stir well and simmer uncovered for 10 minutes.

5 Serve with naan bread and mango chutney.

nutrition facts	
energy	338 cal
	1413 kJ
protein	18 g
fat	16 g
of which saturated	2 g
carbohydrate	33 g
fiber	7 g
cholesterol	0 mg
sodium	403 mg

root vegetable and tofu bake

SERVES 4

2 Tbsp olive oil

9 oz firm tofu

6-8 medium carrots

2 rutabaga

1 parsnip

2 medium firm-fleshed potatoes

¼ cup butter

2 Tbsp cornstarch

1½ cups milk

1½ cups well-flavored vegetable broth

1 tsp dried thyme

Salt and pepper

4 Tbsp grated Gruyère cheese

2 Tbsp grated Parmesan

Slices of garlic and herb bread, to serve

Chopped parsley, to garnish

THE MIX OF VEGETABLES CAN BE VARIED ACCORDING TO WHAT YOU HAVE AVAILABLE BUT ALWAYS INCLUDE A FAIRLY HIGH PROPORTION OF CARROTS AS THESE HAVE THE MOST FLAVOR.

1 Heat the oil in a pan and sauté the tofu until golden brown all over. Drain on paper towels and place in a bowl.

2 Peel the vegetables (except the potatoes) and cut all of them, including the potatoes, into small, even-size chunks. Cook in a pan of boiling water until just tender. Drain and add to the tofu. Spoon into an ovenproof dish.

3 Preheat the oven to 350°F.

4 Heat the butter in a saucepan and stir in the cornstarch. Blend in the milk and broth and bring to a boil, stirring until thickened and smooth. Add the thyme and seasoning, and half the Gruyère. Pour over the vegetables and tofu, and sprinkle with the remaining Gruyère and Parmesan. Bake for 20 to 25 minutes until golden.

5 Serve with slices of garlic and herb bread baked in the oven until crisp. Garnish with chopped parsley.

nutrition facts	
energy	460 cal
	1921 kJ
protein	16 g
fat	27 g
of which saturated	13 g
carbohydrate	40 g
fiber	7 g
cholesterol	51 mg
sodium	515 mg

stuffed mushrooms with smoked tofu, parsley, and garlic

SERVES 4

3 Tbsp extra-virgin olive oil

4 large mushrooms

4 oz smoked tofu, grated

2 large garlic cloves, peeled and finely chopped

⅓ cup fresh whole-wheat breadcrumbs

2 Tbsp chopped fresh parsley

⅓ cup soft goat cheese

1 Tbsp lemon juice

Salt and freshly ground black pepper

¾ cup chicken or vegetable broth

LARGE MUSHROOMS ARE NEEDED FOR THIS DISH, WHICH CAN BE SERVED AS A SIDE DISH, VEGETABLE ACCOMPANIMENT TO GRILLED STEAKS AND CHOPS, OR AS A LIGHT LUNCH OR SUPPER DISH.

1 Heat 2 tablespoons of the olive oil in a skillet, add the mushroom caps, rounded side down, and sauté over a brisk heat for 1 minute to brown. Remove from the pan with a slotted spoon and place in an ovenproof dish.

2 Chop the mushroom stalks and add to the pan with the tofu and garlic. Sauté gently for 5 minutes, then tip into a bowl, and stir in the breadcrumbs, parsley, goat cheese, and lemon juice. Season with salt and pepper and spoon into the mushroom caps, pressing down firmly. Drizzle the rest of the oil over the top of the mushrooms and pour the broth around them.

3 Bake for 20 minutes at 375°F until golden. Serve hot.

nutrition facts	
energy	170 cal
	694 kJ
protein	7 g
fat	13 g
of which saturated	3 g
carbohydrate	6 g
fiber	1 g
cholesterol	0 mg
sodium	341 mg

tofu and **vegetable** biryani

SERVES 4

2 Tbsp peanut oil

2 red onions, peeled and sliced

1 eggplant, peeled and cut into
½-in cubes

1 tsp fresh garlic purée

1 tsp fresh ginger purée

2 tsp cumin seeds

1 tsp ground turmeric

2 tsp ground coriander

2 large carrots, sliced thin

14-oz can chopped tomatoes

1 cup basmati rice

1½ cups vegetable broth

2 cups small cauliflower florets

½ cup green beans, cut into 1-in
lengths

9 oz firm tofu, cubed

3 Tbsp golden raisins

2 Tbsp toasted flaked almonds

2 Tbsp chopped fresh cilantro

IF YOU WANT TO SERVE A SAUCE WITH THIS DRY, RICE-BASED CURRY, SAUTÉ A FINELY CHOPPED ONION WITH A TABLESPOON OF MILD CURRY PASTE, THEN ADD TWO OUNCES OF RED LENTILS, TWO CUPS OF VEGETABLE BROTH, AND TWO CHOPPED TOMATOES. SIMMER THE MIXTURE IN A COVERED PAN FOR 30 MINUTES. RAITA AND NAAN BREAD ARE THE TRADITIONAL ACCOMPANIMENTS.

1 Preheat the oven to 350°F. Heat the oil in a flameproof casserole and sauté the onions, eggplant, garlic, and ginger over a low heat for 10 minutes, stirring occasionally. Add the cumin seeds, turmeric, and coriander, and sauté for 5 more minutes, stirring regularly. Add the carrots and chopped tomatoes. Stir well, then cover the pan, and simmer for 20 minutes.

2 Add the rice, then pour in the broth, and add the cauliflower florets, beans, tofu, and golden raisins.

3 Bring to a simmer, then cover, and cook in the oven for 20 minutes. Remove and leave to stand for 10 minutes without removing the lid from the pan. Fork up the rice, stir in the flaked almonds and cilantro, and serve.

nutrition facts	
energy	490 cal
	2033 kJ
protein	17 g
fat	14 g
of which saturated	1.5 g
carbohydrate	73 g
fiber	7 g
cholesterol	0 mg
sodium	253 mg

bread baskets with tofu and asparagus

SERVES 6

6 large slices of bread, crusts removed

4 Tbsp olive oil

FOR THE FILLING:

1 tsp olive oil

9 oz firm tofu, cut into batons

12 thin asparagus spears, cut into 2-in lengths

½ cup sugar snap peas

1 red bell pepper, seeded and cut into small chunks

FOR THE SAUCE:

1 cup puréed tomatoes

1 Tbsp green olive paste

1 Tbsp balsamic vinegar

1 Tbsp sun-dried tomato paste

Basil leaves, to garnish

THE BREAD BASKETS CAN BE PREPARED IN ADVANCE AND REHEATED FOR FIVE MINUTES IN A HOT OVEN WHEN NEEDED. GRILL THE TOFU AND VEGETABLES IN A RIDGED PAN OR STIR-FRY FOR A FEW MINUTES.

1 Preheat the oven to 375°F. Roll out the bread with a rolling pin until thin, brush the slices on both sides with the olive oil, and press into small basins or cups. Line with wax paper and fill with a few baking beans to keep the "basket" shape and bake in the oven for 10 minutes. Remove the beans and wax paper, and bake for 5 more minutes or until golden and crisp.

2 For the filling, heat a ridged grill pan and, when very hot, drizzle with the olive oil. Add the tofu, asparagus, sugar snap peas, and bell pepper (cook in batches if necessary), and grill for 5 minutes, turning the pieces over once or twice.

3 For the sauce, combine the ingredients in a pan and heat through until hot and thoroughly mixed.

4 To serve, spoon a little sauce onto each serving plate. Place a bread basket alongside, filled with the tofu and vegetables. Garnish with basil leaves and serve.

nutrition facts	
energy	216 cal
	900 kJ
protein	8 g
fat	11 g
of which saturated	1.5 g
carbohydrate	22 g
fiber	2 g
cholesterol	0 mg
sodium	261 mg

singapore noodles

SERVES 4

2 cups thin egg noodles

3 Tbsp vegetable oil

1 yellow bell pepper, seeded and sliced

9 oz firm tofu, cut into small pieces

1 red chile, thinly sliced

½ cup sugar snap peas, cut into halves

4 scallions, chopped

½ tsp fresh ginger purée

1 tsp ground coriander

8 oz green tiger prawns

Juice of 1 lime

2 Tbsp light soy sauce

2 Tbsp hoisin sauce

THE NONYA CUISINE OF SINGAPORE COMBINES ELEMENTS OF BOTH CHINESE AND MALAYSIAN COOKING, DEVELOPING, AS IT DID, WHEN EARLY CHINESE TRADERS SETTLED IN SINGAPORE, PENANG, AND MALACCA, AND MARRIED LOCAL GIRLS. GINGER, LIME, CORIANDER, AND CHILES ARE ALL TRADITIONAL FLAVORS OF NONYA COOKING.

1 Cook the noodles in a large pan of boiling water for 5 minutes or until tender. Drain and toss with 1 tablespoon of the vegetable oil to stop the noodles from sticking together.

2 Heat the remaining oil in a wok, add the bell pepper and tofu, and stir-fry for 5 minutes. Add the chile, sugar snap peas, and scallions, and stir-fry for 5 more minutes.

3 Add the ginger purée, ground coriander, and prawns, and cook for 2 to 3 minutes until the prawns turn pink.

4 Add the noodles, lime juice, soy sauce, and hoisin sauce, and toss together for a few minutes until hot throughout. Serve at once.

nutrition facts	
energy	445 cal
	1871 kJ
protein	26 g
fat	17 g
of which saturated	3 g
carbohydrate	51 g
fiber	3 g
cholesterol	133 mg
sodium	693 mg

roasted **ratatouille** with tofu

SERVES 4

1 each red, yellow, and orange bell peppers, seeded and cut into chunks

1½ cups chestnut mushrooms, cut into quarters

1 green zucchini, cut into chunks

1 yellow zucchini, cut into chunks

1 eggplant, cut into chunks

4 plum tomatoes, cut into quarters lengthwise

9 oz firm tofu, cubed

5 Tbsp extra-virgin olive oil

Freshly ground black pepper

2 Tbsp balsamic vinegar

1 Tbsp fennel seeds

Basil leaves, to garnish

THIS OVEN-ROASTED RATATOUILLE IS TOSSED IN A TANGY VINAIGRETTE OF BALSAMIC VINEGAR AND OLIVE OIL.

1 Preheat the oven to 400°F.

2 Spread out the peppers, mushrooms, zucchini, eggplant, tomatoes, and tofu in a shallow ovenproof baking pan. Drizzle over the olive oil and season with plenty of freshly ground black pepper.

3 Turn the vegetables and tofu over so that they are coated in the oil and roast for 30 to 40 minutes or until the vegetables are tender and scorched at the edges. When they are cooked, transfer to a serving dish, sprinkle over the vinegar and fennel seeds, and serve at once, garnished with basil leaves.

nutrition facts	
energy	210 cal
	871 kJ
protein	7 g
fat	14 g
of which saturated	2 g
carbohydrate	13 g
fiber	5 g
cholesterol	0 mg
sodium	18 mg

tofu, **broccoli**, and **sweet potato** gratin

SERVES 4

2 cups broccoli, divided into small florets and stalks chopped

2 leeks, trimmed and sliced

1 large sweet potato, peeled and cut into 1-in chunks

1 large potato, peeled and cut into ¾-in chunks

1 cup corn kernels

9 oz firm tofu, cubed

14-oz can plum tomatoes, drained and chopped

Salt and freshly ground black pepper

¼ cup butter

½ cup all-purpose flour

1¾ cups milk

1 tsp dried mixed herbs

½ cup grated Cheddar cheese

2 Tbsp grated Parmesan

THIS IS A DISH THAT CAN BE PREPARED WELL IN ADVANCE AND THEN JUST PUT IN THE OVEN TO COOK WHEN REQUIRED.

1 Preheat the oven to 375°F. Cook the broccoli, leeks, sweet potato, and potato in a pan of boiling water for 7 to 8 minutes or until tender. Drain and mix with the corn, tofu, tomatoes, and seasoning. Spoon into an ovenproof dish.

2 Melt the butter in a pan, blend in the flour, and then mix in the milk. Stir until thick and smooth, then add the dried herbs, and spoon over the vegetables and tofu.

3 Sprinkle with the Cheddar and Parmesan, and bake in the oven for 35 to 40 minutes until golden.

nutrition facts	
energy	530 cal
	2229 kJ
protein	25 g
fat	23 g
of which saturated	13 g
carbohydrate	58 g
fiber	7 g
cholesterol	57 mg
sodium	376 mg

smoked tofu **bruschetta**

USE FRENCH BREAD SLICED DIAGONALLY FOR A LARGER
SURFACE AREA OR SLICES OF CIABATTA AS A GOOD BASE FOR
BRUSCHETTA. FRIED BASIL LEAVES MAKE AN UNUSUAL
GARNISH BUT USE FRESH LEAVES, IF PREFERRED.

SERVES 4

7 oz smoked tofu, sliced

2 Tbsp balsamic vinegar

2 tsp pesto

8 slices from a ciabatta loaf

1 large garlic clove, peeled and
   cut in half

4 Tbsp extra-virgin olive oil

4 plum tomatoes, sliced

16 black olives

Fried basil leaves, to garnish

1 Place the tofu slices in a dish. Mix together
the balsamic vinegar and pesto, and spoon
over the tofu. Set aside for 30 minutes.

2 Preheat the oven to 400°F. Rub the ciabatta
slices with the garlic and place on a cookie
sheet. Brush or drizzle with the olive oil and
bake in the oven for 10 minutes until golden
and crisp.

3 Top the bread slices with the tofu and tomato
slices, and the olives. Drizzle over any of the
balsamic mixture left in the dish. Serve
garnished with large basil leaves that have
been deep-fried in hot oil for a few seconds
until crisp and then drained on paper towels.

nutrition facts	
energy	165 cal
	684 kJ
protein	5 g
fat	10 g
of which saturated	1.5 g
carbohydrate	14 g
fiber	1 g
cholesterol	0 mg
sodium	377 mg

red bell **pepper**, tofu, and **corn fritters**

SERVES 4

5 oz smoked tofu, finely diced

⅔ cup corn kernels

1 small red bell pepper, seeded and finely diced

⅔ cup all-purpose flour

2 Tbsp milk

1 large egg

1 Tbsp chopped fresh cilantro

Oil for frying

FOR THE DIP:

½ cup Greek yogurt

½ tsp paprika

IF YOU DON'T HAVE A COOKING THERMOMETER TO CHECK THE TEMPERATURE OF THE OIL, STAND A WOODEN SPOON UPSIDE DOWN IN THE PAN AND WHEN SMALL BUBBLES FORM AROUND THE HANDLE, THE OIL IS READY FOR FRYING.

1 Mix together the tofu, corn kernels, bell pepper, and flour. Beat together the milk and egg and stir into the tofu mixture with the cilantro to make a thick batter.

2 Heat about 2 inches of oil in a wok or other large, deep pan to 350°F. Drop three very scant tablespoonfuls of the mixture into the oil and fry for about 30 seconds on each side until golden brown.

3 Drain with a slotted spoon on paper towels and fry the remaining mixture in the same way to make 12 fritters.

4 For the dip, spoon the yogurt into a bowl and sprinkle the paprika over the top. Serve with the warm fritters.

nutrition facts	
energy	290 cal
	1200 kJ
protein	10 g
fat	19 g
of which saturated	4 g
carbohydrate	21 g
fiber	1.5 g
cholesterol	60 mg
sodium	55 mg

glazed baked **root vegetables** and tofu

SERVES 6

1 large turnip

6 medium carrots

2 medium rutabaga

1 large parsnip

2 large potatoes

9 oz firm tofu

¼ cup butter

1 Tbsp brown sugar

1 tsp Dijon mustard

¾ cup cornstarch

2¾ cups milk

1 tsp chopped fresh thyme leaves

Salt and pepper

4 Tbsp grated Edam or Gruyère cheese

2 Tbsp dry breadcrumbs

LIGHTLY CARAMELIZING THE VEGETABLES AND TOFU WITH BUTTER, BROWN SUGAR, AND MUSTARD GIVES THIS DISH EXTRA FLAVOR. SOME OF THE VEGETABLES COULD BE REPLACED WITH SHREDDED CHICKEN OR COOKED GAMMON, IF YOU LIKE.

1 Peel the vegetables and cut into small, even-size chunks. Cut the tofu into similar-size pieces. Cook the vegetables in a large pan of boiling water until just tender. Drain, add the butter, sugar, and mustard to the pan and, when melted, tip the vegetables back in, add the tofu, and stir with a wooden spoon until coated. Set aside.

2 Preheat the oven to 350°F.

3 In a bowl, mix the cornstarch with a little of the milk until blended. Heat the rest of the milk in a pan with the thyme and, when almost at a boil, pour onto the cornstarch mixture, stirring continuously. Return to the pan and stir over a low heat until thickened and smooth. Season, stir in half the cheese, then pour over the vegetables and stir to coat. Spoon the mixture into an ovenproof dish.

4 Sprinkle with the remaining cheese and breadcrumbs, and bake for 20 to 25 minutes until crusty on top.

nutrition facts	
energy	344 cal
	1448 kJ
protein	13 g
fat	12 g
of which saturated	5 g
carbohydrate	49 g
fiber	6 g
cholesterol	33 mg
sodium	272 mg

bell **pepper**, tofu, and zucchini **satays**

SERVES 4

9 oz firm tofu, cubed

4 Tbsp crunchy peanut butter

¾ cup Greek yogurt

1 red bell pepper, seeded and cut into chunks

1 large zucchini, cut into chunks

2 Tbsp sunflower oil

FOR THE DIP:

1 Tbsp sunflower oil

4 scallions, chopped

½ red or orange bell pepper, seeded and finely chopped

1 garlic clove, peeled and crushed

Few drops of Tabasco sauce

1 dill pickle, finely chopped

1½ cups tomato pasta sauce

1 tsp dried oregano

Salt and pepper

ALL SUPERMARKETS SELL A WIDE RANGE OF PASTA SAUCES. CHOOSE A CHUNKY TOMATO ONE FOR THE DIPPING SAUCE TO ACCOMPANY THESE SATAYS.

1 Place the tofu cubes in a shallow dish. Mix together the peanut butter and yogurt, spoon over the tofu, and stir until coated. Set aside for 30 minutes. Thread the tofu onto thin skewers alternately with the pepper and zucchini chunks and place on an aluminum foil-lined broiler rack. Spoon over any peanut butter mix left in the dish and brush the vegetables with the sunflower oil.

2 For the dip, heat the oil in a pan and sauté the scallions, pepper and garlic until softened. Add the Tabasco, gherkin, pasta sauce, oregano, and seasoning, and simmer for 10 to 15 minutes or until the excess liquid has evaporated.

3 Meanwhile, broil the skewers for 10 minutes, turning over once or twice until browned. Serve hot with the dip.

nutrition facts	
energy	340 cal
	1421 kJ
protein	12 g
fat	27 g
of which saturated	6 g
carbohydrate	12 g
fiber	3 g
cholesterol	8 mg
sodium	341 mg

pad **thai**

SERVES 4

Peanut oil, for shallow-frying

9 oz firm tofu, cut into 1-in cubes

12-14 raw shrimp, peeled

2 cups flat rice noodles

8 scallions, sliced

2 cups shiitake mushrooms, sliced

¼ cup bean sprouts

2 garlic cloves, peeled and crushed

2 red chiles, seeded and chopped

2 Tbsp smooth peanut butter

3 Tbsp dark soy sauce

Juice of 2 limes

1 Tbsp brown sugar

4 Tbsp vegetable broth or water

Sliced scallion tops, to garnish

ONE OF THAILAND'S MOST FAMOUS AND POPULAR NOODLE DISHES. THE SPELLING MAY CHANGE FROM "PAD" TO "PHAT" THAI AND THERE WILL BE AS MANY VARIATIONS OF THE RECIPE AS THERE ARE COOKS!

1 Heat ¼ inch peanut oil in a wok and, when hot, add the tofu cubes in two batches and fry for about 5 minutes until golden. Drain on paper towels and set aside. Add the shrimp to the wok and fry until they turn pink. Drain on paper towels and set aside.

2 Meanwhile, cook the noodles in a pan of boiling water for 5 minutes or according to the package instructions. Drain, cool under cold water, and pat dry with paper towels.

3 Drain all but 2 tablespoons of the oil from the wok, add the scallions, and mushrooms, and stir-fry for 2 to 3 minutes. Add the bean sprouts, garlic, and chiles, and stir-fry for 2 minutes.

4 Mix together the peanut butter, soy sauce, lime juice, sugar, and broth or water, and pour into the pan. Add the noodles, tofu, and shrimp, and toss over the heat until the noodles are well coated with the sauce and everything has heated through.

5 Sprinkle with the scallion tops and serve immediately.

nutrition facts	
energy	540 cal
	2250 kJ
protein	21 g
fat	30 g
of which saturated	5 g
carbohydrate	46 g
fiber	3 g
cholesterol	100 mg
sodium	853 mg

vegetarian puff slice

SERVES 6

1 Tbsp olive oil

1 red bell pepper, seeded and chopped

9 oz firm tofu, cut into small cubes

14-oz can flageolet beans, drained and rinsed

9-oz can whole chestnuts, drained and chopped

1 tsp fresh rosemary leaves, finely chopped

1 lb puff pastry

2 Tbsp mango chutney

1 cup mozzarella cheese, cubed

Beaten egg, to glaze

2 Tbsp fennel seeds

IT IS A GOOD IDEA TO COOK IT ON A COOKIE SHEET WITH A RAISED EDGE TO PREVENT ANY CHEESE THAT BUBBLES OUT DURING BAKING MAKING A MESS.

1 Heat the oil in a pan and sauté the bell pepper and tofu for about 5 minutes until the pepper has softened. Transfer to a bowl and stir in the beans, chopped chestnuts, and rosemary.

2 Roll out just under half the pastry to a 12 x 9-inch rectangle and lift onto a cookie sheet. Spread the pastry with the mango chutney to within 1 inch of the edges. Spoon over the tofu mixture and top with the mozzarella cubes. Dampen the pastry edges with water.

3 Roll out the rest of the pastry to a slightly larger rectangle and cut into 1-inch diagonal strips. Arrange the strips side by side over the filling. Press the pastry edges together firmly with a fork to seal. Chill the slice for 30 minutes.

4 Preheat the oven to 400°F. Brush the pastry with beaten egg, sprinkle with the fennel seeds, and bake for 40 minutes until puffed and golden brown.

nutrition facts	
energy	600 cal
	2514 kJ
protein	22 g
fat	32 g
of which saturated	5 g
carbohydrate	61 g
fiber	6 g
cholesterol	22 mg
sodium	764 mg

tofu **tortilla**

SERVES 4

2 Tbsp olive oil

9 oz firm tofu, cut into small cubes

1 tsp smoked paprika

1 yellow or orange bell pepper, seeded and chopped

1 zucchini, sliced

6 chorizo sausages, peeled and cut into small chunks

3 plum tomatoes, peeled, seeded, and chopped

½ cup frozen peas

8 large eggs

2 Tbsp snipped fresh chives

Salt and freshly ground black pepper

SERVE WITH A MIXED-LEAF SALAD FOR A SUSTAINING LUNCH OR SUPPER. SERVE COLD, IN SMALL WEDGES, AS A PARTY SNACK.

1 Heat half the oil in a large skillet, add the tofu, and sprinkle over the smoked paprika. Fry for 5 minutes until the tofu browns on all sides. Remove from the pan and set aside. Add the rest of the oil to the pan with the bell pepper, zucchini, and chorizo, and fry for 10 minutes, stirring occasionally. Add the chopped tomatoes and frozen peas, and return the tofu to the pan.

2 Beat the eggs with the chives, season with salt and pepper, and pour into the pan. Cook over a low heat for 7 to 8 minutes until the base is set and beginning to brown (check this by lifting the edges with a round-blade knife).

3 Preheat the broiler. When the base of the tortilla is cooked, slide the pan under the broiler to cook the top. Check that the center is firm by cutting into it with a sharp knife.

4 Serve at once or leave until cold.

nutrition facts	
energy	568 cal
	2357 kJ
protein	32 g
fat	45 g
of which saturated	5 g
carbohydrate	9 g
fiber	2 g
cholesterol	521 mg
sodium	1112 mg

eggplants stuffed with **ham** and smoked tofu

SERVES 4

2 large eggplants

2 Tbsp olive oil

Freshly ground black pepper

FOR THE STUFFING:

1 Tbsp olive oil

1¾ cups mushrooms, sliced

1 leek, sliced thin

7 oz smoked tofu, cut into small cubes

⅔ cup bulgur wheat

1½ cups vegetable broth

2 sun-dried tomatoes, chopped

2 slices of ham, chopped

¾ cup grated Cheddar cheese

½ cup dried roasted peanuts, chopped

2 Tbsp chopped fresh parsley

WHEN HOLLOWING OUT THE EGGPLANT SHELLS, LEAVE A THIN BORDER OF FLESH TO SUPPORT THE SKINS SO THEY DO NOT COLLAPSE WHEN YOU FILL THEM. THE SKINS ARE QUITE THIN AND FRAGILE SO TAKE CARE NOT TO SPLIT THEM WHEN YOU SCOOP OUT THE FLESH.

1 Preheat the oven to 350°F. Cut the eggplants in half lengthwise and score the flesh with a sharp knife. Place in a shallow baking pan, flesh side up, brush with the olive oil, and season with black pepper. Roast them in the oven for 40 minutes or until the flesh is tender.

2 Fifteen minutes before the eggplants are ready, make the stuffing. Heat the oil in a skillet, and sauté the mushrooms and leek for 5 minutes. Add the tofu and bulgur wheat, and pour in the broth. Simmer for about 10 minutes or until the wheat has absorbed the liquid.

3 Remove the eggplant halves from the oven, spoon out the flesh, and add to the tofu mixture with the sun-dried tomatoes and ham.

4 Fill the eggplant halves with the stuffing mixture, pressing it down lightly. Mix together the cheese, chopped peanuts, and parsley, and sprinkle over the top. Return to the oven for 5 minutes or until the cheese melts and bubbles.

nutrition facts	
energy	430 cal
	1800 kJ
protein	20 g
fat	27 g
of which saturated	7 g
carbohydrate	27 g
fiber	6 g
cholesterol	19 mg
sodium	589 mg

penne with piquant
tomato and tofu sauce

SERVES 4

2 Tbsp olive oil

½ cup pine nuts

2 large red bell peppers, seeded and chopped

1 red chile, seeded and finely chopped

9 oz firm tofu, cubed

1 Tbsp balsamic vinegar

1 Tbsp white wine vinegar

1 tsp sugar

1½ cups tomato pasta sauce

4 cups dried penne

Salt and freshly ground black pepper

ALL LARGE SUPERMARKETS SELL A RANGE OF READY-MADE PASTA SAUCES, SO FINDING A WELL-FLAVORED TOMATO ONE SHOULD BE EASY. SUBSTITUTE 12 OUNCES OF PEELED, SEEDED, AND CHOPPED FRESH TOMATOES INSTEAD IF YOU LIKE.

1 Heat the oil in a large skillet and cook the pine nuts until golden brown. Remove from the pan with a slotted spoon and drain on paper towels.

2 Add the peppers and chile to the pan and cook over a fairly high heat until the peppers are soft and scorched at the edges.

3 Add the tofu, balsamic vinegar, wine vinegar, and sugar, and cook for 5 more minutes, stirring occasionally. Add the tomato sauce and leave to simmer gently while you cook the pasta.

4 Bring a large pan of water to a boil, add the penne, and cook for 8 to 10 minutes until *al dente* (firm to the bite) or according to the package instructions. Drain, and mix the penne with the sauce, tossing until coated.

5 Season and serve with the pine nuts scattered over the penne.

nutrition facts	
energy	550 cal
	2323 kJ
protein	20 g
fat	20 g
of which saturated	2 g
carbohydrate	78 g
fiber	5 g
cholesterol	0 mg
sodium	376 mg

tomato, feta, and tofu moussaka

SERVES 4

2 large potatoes, cut into ¼-in slices

1 large carrot, peeled and sliced

1 red onion, peeled, cut into wedges, and layers separated

1 fennel bulb, sliced thin

1 red bell pepper, seeded and chopped

1 zucchini, coarsely chopped

1 eggplant, sliced

9 oz firm tofu, cubed

3 garlic cloves, peeled and sliced

4 Tbsp olive oil

Salt and freshly ground black pepper

14-oz can chopped tomatoes with herbs

2 eggs, beaten

¾ cup natural yogurt

½ cup feta cheese, crumbled

¾ cup mature Cheddar cheese, grated

A VEGETARIAN VERSION OF THE GREEK DISH THAT IS TRADITIONALLY MADE WITH GROUND LAMB. ROASTING THE VEGETABLES FIRST BRINGS OUT THEIR FLAVORS AND ALSO CUTS DOWN ON THE TIME THE ASSEMBLED DISH NEEDS IN THE OVEN.

1 Cook the potatoes and carrot in a pan of boiling water for 5 minutes and then drain.

2 Preheat the oven to 400°F.

3 Spread out all the fresh vegetables, the tofu, and the garlic in a large shallow roasting pan, drizzle with the olive oil, and season with salt and pepper. (If you do not have a large enough pan, divide the mixture between two pans and swap their positions in the oven halfway through the cooking time.) Cook in the oven for 45 minutes, turning the vegetables and tofu over occasionally.

4 Mix the roasted vegetables and tofu with the chopped tomatoes and spoon into an ovenproof dish. Beat together the eggs and yogurt, stir in the feta and Cheddar, and spoon over the mixture.

5 Cook in the oven for 20 to 25 minutes until golden and bubbling.

nutrition facts	
energy	526 cal
	2196 kJ
protein	26 g
fat	31 g
of which saturated	11 g
carbohydrate	38 g
fiber	7 g
cholesterol	196 mg
sodium	643 mg

egg **fried rice** with tofu and **bacon**

SERVES 4

1¾ cups long-grain rice

1 Tbsp peanut oil

3 slices of lean bacon, chopped

8 shallots, peeled and chopped

1 celery rib, chopped

9 oz firm tofu, cut into small
   pieces

1 cup frozen peas

1 tsp fresh ginger purée

9 oz small peeled shrimp

2 Tbsp soy sauce

1 Tbsp oyster sauce

3 eggs, beaten

A CHINESE RESTAURANT OR TAKEAWAY FAVORITE, THIS IS EASY TO COOK AT HOME AND VERY QUICK IF YOU HAVE LEFTOVER RICE. IF YOU LIKE THINGS SPICY, ADD A THINLY SLICED GREEN CHILE WITH THE SHALLOTS.

1 Cook the rice in a pan of boiling water for 10 minutes or until tender. Drain in a colander and pour hot water through the grains to remove any excess starch. Spread out the rice in a shallow tray and dry it off in a 350°F oven for 20 minutes, turning over the grains every 5 minutes.

2 Heat the oil in a wok and fry the bacon and shallots for 5 minutes until lightly browned. Add the celery and tofu and stir-fry for 5 minutes. Stir in the peas and ginger, cook for a couple of minutes, then stir in the rice, shrimp, soy sauce, and oyster sauce. Toss over the heat for 5 minutes.

3 Pour in the beaten eggs and continue to cook for a few minutes until the eggs have set. Serve at once.

nutrition facts	
energy	560 cal
	2357 kJ
protein	35 g
fat	13 g
of which saturated	3 g
carbohydrate	76 g
fiber	1.5 g
cholesterol	304 mg
sodium	987 mg

chili tofu hash browns with bell **peppers**

SERVES 4

2 medium potatoes

2 Tbsp sunflower oil

1 Tbsp chili powder

9 oz firm tofu, cut into small
   cubes

1 red bell pepper, seeded and
   cut into small chunks

1 green bell pepper, seeded and
   cut into small chunks

1¼ cups baby button mushrooms

Freshly ground black pepper

2 Tbsp chopped fresh parsley

1 Tbsp finely chopped fresh
   rosemary leaves

LEAVE THE SKINS ON THE POTATOES FOR EXTRA TEXTURE AND FLAVOR, AND USE EITHER NEW OR MAIN-CROP POTATOES AS YOU PREFER. BLANCHING THEM FIRST SHORTENS THE TIME THEY NEED IN THE SKILLET.

1 Scrub the potatoes and cut into roughly ¾-inch chunks. Cook in a pan of boiling water for 5 minutes and then drain.

2 Heat the oil in a large skillet, add the potatoes, and sprinkle over the chili powder. Fry over a medium heat until the potatoes are starting to brown, then add the tofu, bell peppers, and mushrooms. Season with plenty of black pepper and fry for 10 more minutes or until the vegetables are tender. Scatter over the chopped herbs and serve as an accompaniment to poached or scrambled eggs, broiled fish, or steak.

nutrition facts	
energy	200 cal
	826 kJ
protein	9 g
fat	9 g
of which saturated	1 g
carbohydrate	22 g
fiber	3 g
cholesterol	0 mg
sodium	15 mg

tuna tofu niçoise

GRILL THE TUNA AND TOFU CONVENTIONALLY OR COOK IN A
RIDGED GRIDDLE PAN. MAKE SURE THE PAN IS REALLY HOT
BEFORE ADDING A LITTLE OLIVE OIL AND THEN THE FISH AND
TOFU. IF THE FOOD STICKS INITIALLY, LEAVE IT TO COOK OVER
A HIGH HEAT FOR A MINUTE OR TWO, BY WHICH TIME IT WILL
HAVE SEALED AND RELEASED ITSELF FROM THE PAN.

SERVES 4

¼ cup green beans

½ cup olive oil

4 Tbsp lemon juice

Salt and freshly ground black
   pepper

1 Tbsp chopped fresh oregano

12 baby plum tomatoes, cut into
   halves

1 red onion, peeled and finely
   chopped

¾ cup cucumber, sliced

½ cup black olives

9 oz fresh tuna steak

9 oz firm tofu, frozen and
   defrosted

Lemon wedges, to serve

1 Cook the green beans in a pan of boiling water for 2 minutes. Drain and refresh by running cold water over them.

2 Reserve 1 tablespoon olive oil and put the rest in a large bowl with the lemon juice, salt, pepper, and oregano. Whisk together until combined then add the beans, tomato halves, chopped onion, cucumber, and olives. Toss lightly to coat with the dressing, then set aside.

3 Slice the tuna and tofu into 2-inch strips and season. Heat a ridged griddle pan and, when really hot, add the reserved olive oil. Cook the tuna and tofu in batches for 1 to 2 minutes on each side, depending on thickness. If using a conventional broiler, preheat it, brush the tuna and tofu with the oil, and place on an aluminum foil-lined rack. Cook as close to the heat as possible.

4 Spoon the bean salad onto serving plates and serve with the hot tuna and tofu. Pour over any dressing left in the bowl and serve with lemon wedges.

nutrition facts	
energy	340 cal
	1418 kJ
protein	22 g
fat	25 g
of which saturated	4 g
carbohydrate	7 g
fiber	2 g
cholesterol	18 mg
sodium	323 mg

5 drinks and desserts

In this chapter you will discover tofu treats for all the family. Younger children will delight in the thick shakes and smoothies and banana fritters, while the most stylish of dinner parties could be graced with the dark chocolate tart or rich vanilla creams. From ice dishes to rice dishes, you will find a delectable selection of imaginative tofu recipes for the sweetest part of the meal.

LEFT vanilla tofu creams with gingered black currant coulis (page 140)

mango and tofu brûlées

1 large mango, peeled and flesh chopped, or 9 oz prepared chopped mango

½ cup low-fat crème fraîche

7 oz firm tofu

Finely grated rind of 1 lime

4 Tbsp raw brown sugar

Fine shreds of lime zest, to decorate

SCORCH THE TOPS OF THESE CREAMY DESSERTS WITH A SMALL GAS BLOWTORCH, SO POPULAR WITH TV CHEFS OR, IF YOU DON'T HAVE ONE, A CONVENTIONAL BROILER WILL WORK JUST AS WELL.

1 Preheat the broiler.

2 Divide the chopped mango among four individual heatproof dishes.

3 Purée the crème fraîche, tofu, and lime rind together in a food processor, or mash the tofu and stir in the crème fraîche and lime rind.

4 Spoon over the fruit in an even layer. Sprinkle the sugar on top to cover completely, and place under a very hot broiler for a few minutes until the sugar melts and caramelizes. Decorate with lime zest, and serve.

nutrition facts	
energy	200 cal
	850 kJ
protein	2.5 g
fat	11 g
of which saturated	5 g
carbohydrate	25 g
fiber	1.5 g
cholesterol	0 mg
sodium	3 mg

phyllo cigars filled with **honey**, tofu, and **apricots**

SERVES 4

1 cup no-soak dried apricots, finely chopped

3 oz firm tofu, crumbled or mashed with a fork

½ cup pistachios, finely chopped

1 Tbsp liquid honey

1 tsp finely grated lemon zest

8 sheets phyllo pastry

Sunflower oil, for brushing

Confectioners' sugar, to dust

SERVE THESE CRISP PHYLLO PASTRIES WITH NATURAL GREEK YOGURT AND A LITTLE EXTRA HONEY DRIZZLED OVER, IF YOU LIKE.

1 Preheat the oven to 375°F. In a bowl, mix together the apricots, tofu, pistachios, honey, and lemon zest.

2 Lay one sheet of phyllo pastry on the work surface and brush lightly with sunflower oil. Spoon one-eighth of the tofu mixture down the center and roll the pastry around it, tucking in the ends, to make a long, thin cigar.

3 Repeat with the remaining phyllo and filling. Place on a cookie sheet, brush with a little more sunflower oil, and bake for 15 minutes until crisp and golden. Dust with confectioners' sugar and serve warm.

nutrition facts	
energy	288 cal
	1205 kJ
protein	8 g
fat	14 g
of which saturated	2 g
carbohydrate	34 g
fiber	5 g
cholesterol	0 mg
sodium	74 mg

dark **chocolate** and tofu **tart**

SERVES 10–12

FOR THE BASE:

2 cups chocolate cream cookies

¼ cup ground hazelnuts

6 Tbsp butter, melted

FOR THE FILLING:

1 packet of gelatin

¼ cup fresh orange juice

6 oz dark chocolate

9 oz soft tofu

½ cup superfine sugar

1¼ cups heavy cream, for whipping

TO DECORATE:

Chocolate curls or shavings

Fresh raspberries

Cocoa powder and powdered sugar, to dust

USE DARK CHOCOLATE WITH AROUND 70 PERCENT COCOA SOLIDS FOR A REALLY STRONG CHOCOLATEY FLAVOR.

1 For the base, crush the cookies to crumbs, then mix with the ground hazelnuts and melted butter. Press over the base and up the sides of a 9-inch pie plate. Chill for 1 hour.

2 For the filling, in a small bowl, sprinkle the gelatin over the orange juice. Allow to stand for a few minutes, then dissolve in the microwave for 3 to 4 minutes on defrost setting, or stand the bowl in a pan of hot water, to soften the gelatin.

3 Chop the chocolate into small pieces and place in a mixing bowl. Stand the bowl over a pan of hot water and leave until melted. Stir in the dissolved gelatin.

4 Purée the tofu with half the sugar and stir in to the chocolate. Whip the cream with the rest of the sugar until standing in soft peaks and stir into the chocolate mixture a little at a time until evenly blended.

5 Chill until starting to thicken, stirring occasionally, then spoon into the cookie case and chill until firmly set.

6 Decorate with chocolate curls or shavings and a few raspberries. Sift over a dusting of cocoa powder and powdered sugar just before serving.

nutrition facts per slice	
energy	350 cal
	1470 kJ
protein	4 g
fat	25 g
of which saturated	12 g
carbohydrate	29 g
fiber	1 g
cholesterol	49 mg
sodium	92 mg

tofu and **banana** fritters with toffee sauce

SERVES 4

1 large ripe banana

9 oz firm tofu

⅔ cup all-purpose flour

2 Tbsp milk

1 large egg

Oil for deep-frying

FOR THE TOFFEE SAUCE:

½ cup superfine sugar

½ cup sweet butter

Juice of ½ lemon

½ cup Greek yogurt

IF YOU WANT TO AVOID THE CALORIES IN THE TOFFEE SAUCE, SERVE THE FRITTERS WITH A RASPBERRY OR APRICOT COULIS INSTEAD. MAKE SURE THE OIL IS REALLY HOT BEFORE YOU ADD THE FRITTERS SO THAT THEY COOK QUICKLY AND ABSORB AS LITTLE OIL AS POSSIBLE.

1 In a bowl, coarsely mash the banana and tofu together. Stir in the flour. Beat together the milk and egg, and stir in to make a thick batter.

2 Heat the oil for deep-frying to 350°F. Drop three half-tablespoonfuls of the mixture into the oil and fry for about 30 seconds on each side until golden brown. Drain with a slotted spoon onto paper towels and fry the remaining mixture in the same way to make 12 fritters.

3 For the sauce, melt the sugar and butter together in a pan, and bring to a boil. Stir continuously until the mixture turns a rich brown color, then take off the heat and add the lemon juice. Gradually stir in the yogurt.

4 Serve the fritters with the warm sauce poured over them.

nutrition facts	
energy	580 cal
	2431 kJ
protein	11 g
fat	39 g
of which saturated	17 g
carbohydrate	51 g
fiber	1 g
cholesterol	117 mg
sodium	234 mg

baked yogurt **cheesecake** with honey apricots

SERVES 6

FOR THE BASE:

3 cups graham crackers, crushed

¼ cup pecans, finely chopped

3 Tbsp porridge oats

¼ cup butter, melted

FOR THE TOPPING:

1 cup curd or ricotta cheese

9 oz firm tofu

1¼ cups Greek yogurt

3 large eggs

½ cup brown sugar

1 tsp vanilla extract

FOR THE APRICOTS:

¾ cup ready-to-eat dried apricots, chopped

4 Tbsp honey

1 Tbsp fresh lemon juice

½ cup pecans, coarsely chopped

AS IT COOLS, THE CHEESECAKE WILL CRACK BUT LEAVING IT IN THE TURNED-OFF OVEN AND RUNNING A KNIFE AROUND THE EDGE TO LOOSEN IT FROM THE PAN WILL HELP TO MINIMIZE THIS. ANY CRACKS THAT DO APPEAR WILL BE COVERED BY THE YOGURT SPREAD OVER THE CHEESECAKE BEFORE SERVING, SO DON'T WORRY TOO MUCH ABOUT THEM!

1 To make the base, mix the crushed graham crackers, pecans, and oats together in a bowl, and stir in the melted butter. Press over the base of an 8-inch springform pan and chill in the refrigerator while you prepare the topping.

2 Preheat the oven to 325°F.

3 To make the topping, put the curd cheese, tofu, ½ cup of the yogurt, eggs, sugar, and vanilla in a food processor and blend until creamy. If you don't have a food processor, mash the tofu in a bowl and then beat in the other ingredients.

4 Pour over the base, place on a cookie sheet, and bake in the oven for 30 to 35 minutes until just firm. Remove and run a knife around the cheesecake to loosen it from the pan, then return to the switched-off oven, and leave to cool. When cold, chill for 3 to 4 hours.

5 Carefully remove from the pan and place on a serving plate. Spread the top with the rest of the yogurt. Warm the apricots with the honey, lemon juice, and pecans, and serve spooned over the cheesecake.

nutrition facts	
energy	730 cal
	3056 kJ
protein	15 g
fat	51 g
of which saturated	21 g
carbohydrate	56 g
fiber	4 g
cholesterol	177 mg
sodium	451 mg

raspberry, orange, and tofu trifles

SERVES 6

6 trifle sponges

6 Tbsp sweet sherry or muscat wine

2 cups raspberries

5 oz firm tofu

4 Tbsp mascarpone cheese

1 Tbsp honey

Finely grated rind of 1 orange

1⅓ cups thick custard

4 Tbsp chopped toasted hazelnuts

Small sprigs of mint and red currants or orange zest, to decorate

CHILL THESE FOR SEVERAL HOURS SO THAT THE FRUIT FLAVORS CAN DEVELOP AND MINGLE. OTHER FRUITS COULD BE USED INSTEAD OF RASPBERRIES, SUCH AS STRAWBERRIES, BLUEBERRIES, OR PITTED CHERRIES.

1 Roughly chop the trifle sponges and divide half among six small dishes or tumblers. Spoon over 4 tablespoons of the sherry or muscat wine and add a layer of raspberries.

2 Liquidize the tofu, mascarpone, honey, orange rind, and remaining sherry or wine, or mash the tofu and mix with the other ingredients.

3 Build up the trifles adding alternate spoonfuls of custard, tofu mixture, sponge fingers, and raspberries until all have been used up, finishing with raspberries and tofu.

4 Sprinkle the toasted hazelnuts over the top and decorate with mint and orange zest.

nutrition facts	
energy	300 cal
	1300 kJ
protein	9 g
fat	16 g
of which saturated	4 g
carbohydrate	29 g
fiber	2 g
cholesterol	75 mg
sodium	100 mg

caramelized tofu rice

SERVES 6

A little sunflower oil, for greasing

1½ cups milk

5 oz soft tofu

½ cup flaked rice

1 cup superfine sugar

1 tsp vanilla extract

2 large eggs, separated

Stewed fruit, to serve

AN EASY WAY TO TURN A SIMPLE RICE PUDDING INTO SOMETHING MORE SPECIAL. SERVE THE INDIVIDUAL PUDDINGS WARM WITH STEWED LATE-SUMMER FRUITS SUCH AS BLACKBERRIES, PLUMS, OR APPLES AND PEARS.

1 Brush six 5-fluid-ounce ovenproof basins or cups lightly with sunflower oil. Liquidize the milk and tofu together, and pour into a pan. Add the rice and half the sugar, and bring to a gentle simmer. Lower the heat and cook gently for about 15 minutes until the mixture is thick and creamy. Stir in the vanilla and leave to cool.

2 Preheat the oven to 300°F. Heat the remaining sugar in a heavy-based pan with 6 tablespoons of water. When dissolved, bring to a boil and cook until it is a rich caramel color. Pour immediately into the basins, tilting them so that the base and sides are coated.

3 Stir the egg yolks into the rice mixture. Whisk the whites until they are stiff, fold them into the mixture, and spoon it into the basins.

4 Lift the basins into a roasting pan and pour in 1 inch of hot water. Bake uncovered in the oven for 30 minutes or until the mixture is just firm. Turn out onto serving plates and serve warm with stewed fruit.

nutrition facts	
energy	260 cal
	1111 kJ
protein	7.5 g
fat	6 g
of which saturated	2 g
carbohydrate	46 g
fiber	0 g
cholesterol	86 mg
sodium	62 mg

praline tofu ice cream

IF YOU DO NOT HAVE AN ICE-CREAM MAKER, FREEZE THE MIXTURE UNTIL IT IS SLUSHY, THEN TRANSFER TO A BOWL AND WHISK BEFORE RETURNING TO THE FREEZER. LET THE ICE CREAM SOFTEN A LITTLE BEFORE SERVING.

SERVES 6

Oil, for greasing

⅔ cup granulated sugar

1 cup unblanched almonds

1 cup Greek yogurt

9 oz firm tofu

¼ cup superfine sugar

1½ cups heavy cream, for whipping

1 Lightly grease an aluminum foil-lined cookie sheet. Put the granulated sugar and the almonds in a heavy-based pan and heat very gently until the sugar melts and turns a rich caramel color.

2 Pour the nuts and caramel onto the cookie sheet and leave until cold and hard. Lift off and grind coarsely in a food processor or food mill.

3 Purée together the yogurt, tofu, superfine sugar, and cream, or mash the tofu and mix in the other ingredients. Stir in the crushed praline (nut and caramel mixture).

4 Freeze in an ice-cream maker according to the manufacturer's instructions, then pack into a freezer container and freeze until solid. Alternatively, place in the freezer until slushy, break up and whisk well before packing into a container and freezing.

5 Serve in scoops on its own or with fresh fruit.

nutrition facts	
energy	500 cal
	2077 kJ
protein	10 g
fat	35 g
of which saturated	15 g
carbohydrate	40 g
fiber	1 g
cholesterol	53 mg
sodium	54 mg

strawberry tofu mousse

IF STRAWBERRIES ARE IN SEASON AND THEREFORE SWEET AND AROMATIC, YOU WILL ONLY NEED TO ADD A VERY LITTLE SUGAR TO THE MOUSSE, SO TASTE THE MIXTURE BEFORE DECIDING ON HOW MUCH. THE RECIPE COULD ALSO BE MADE USING MANGOES, BLUEBERRIES, OR FRESH, RIPE APRICOTS.

SERVES 6

4 cups fresh strawberries

9 oz firm tofu

¼ cup superfine sugar (or to taste)

Finely grated zest and juice of 1 lemon

1 packet of gelatin

¾ cup heavy cream, whipped

Mint sprigs, to decorate

1 Set aside six strawberries for decoration and hull the rest. Coarsely chop and place in a food processor with the tofu, sugar, and lemon zest, and whizz to make a smooth purée. Transfer to a bowl.

2 Put the lemon juice in a small bowl and sprinkle the gelatin over it. Leave to stand for 5 minutes, then dissolve by standing the bowl in a pan of hot water.

3 Stir into the strawberry purée and then fold in all but 2 tablespoonfuls of the cream. Taste for sweetness and stir in a little more sugar if necessary.

4 Spoon the mousse into a large serving bowl or six individual dishes and chill until set. Serve decorated with blobs of the reserved cream, the whole strawberries, and mint sprigs.

nutrition facts	
energy	185 cal
	772 kJ
protein	7 g
fat	12 g
of which saturated	6 g
carbohydrate	14 g
fiber	1 g
cholesterol	26 mg
sodium	24 mg

vanilla tofu creams with gingered black currant coulis

SERVES 4

FOR THE COULIS:

3 cups black currants

½ cup water

¼ cup superfine sugar

½ tsp ground ginger

FOR THE CREAMS:

1 packet of gelatin

9 oz soft tofu

¾ cup milk

¼ cup superfine sugar

1 cup heavy cream, for whipping

1 tsp vanilla extract

Mint sprigs, to garnish

BLACKBERRIES, RASPBERRIES, BLUEBERRIES, OR APRICOTS COULD ALL BE USED INSTEAD OF BLACK CURRANTS TO MAKE THE COULIS.

1 For the coulis, strip the black currants from their stalks, reserving a few for decoration. Place in a pan with the water, sugar, and ginger, and simmer for 10 to 15 minutes until soft. Liquidize or push through a sieve.

2 For the creams, sprinkle the gelatin over 2 tablespoons cold water in a small bowl. Stand the bowl in a pan of hot water and leave until dissolved. Allow to cool. Liquidize the tofu with the milk and sugar until smooth. Transfer to a bowl and stir in the gelatin.

3 In another bowl whip the cream with the vanilla until standing in soft peaks, then fold into the tofu mixture. Chill until starting to thicken, stirring occasionally.

4 Lightly grease four individual pudding basins and divide the mixture among them. Chill until firmly set.

5 To serve, loosen the creams from the basins and turn out onto serving plates. Spoon the coulis around and decorate with the reserved black currants and mint sprigs.

nutrition facts	
energy	400 cal
	1665 kJ
protein	10 g
fat	25 g
of which saturated	13 g
carbohydrate	36 g
fiber	3 g
cholesterol	60 mg
sodium	47 mg

tofu pancakes with blueberries and maple syrup

SERVES 6

1⅔ cups self-rising flour

1 tsp ground cinnamon

2 Tbsp superfine sugar

2 large eggs

4 oz firm tofu

¾ cup buttermilk

2 Tbsp butter, melted

A little sunflower oil, for greasing

FOR THE TOPPING:

Blueberries

Maple syrup

FOR BEST RESULTS, COOK THE PANCAKES IN A HEAVY, NONSTICK SKILLET, HEATING THE PAN THOROUGHLY BEFORE YOU ADD THE MIXTURE. ONCE COOKED, WRAP THE PANCAKES IN A CLEAN DISH TOWEL SO THAT THEY STAY WARM AND SOFT.

1 Sift the flour and cinnamon into a bowl and stir in the sugar. Liquidize the eggs, tofu, and buttermilk together, and gradually whisk into the dry ingredients until smooth. Stir in the melted butter.

2 Heat a heavy, nonstick skillet or griddle, and grease with a little sunflower oil. Spoon 3 or 4 tablespoons of the mixture into the pan and cook for about 3 minutes until browned underneath and bubbles appear on the surface.

3 Flip over and brown the other side. Remove from the pan and keep warm wrapped in a clean dish towel while you cook the rest of the pancakes.

4 Serve warm with blueberries and a drizzle of maple syrup.

nutrition facts	
energy	217 cal
	912 kJ
protein	18 g
fat	7 g
of which saturated	3 g
carbohydrate	32 g
fiber	1 g
cholesterol	88 mg
sodium	75 mg

RIGHT vanilla tofu creams with gingered black currant coulis

strawberry, banana, and tofu smoothie

SERVES 2–3

1 medium banana, peeled and chopped

1¼ cups strawberries, hulled and chopped

5 oz soft tofu

2 Tbsp liquid honey

1¾ cups low-fat milk

Ground cinnamon and whole strawberries, to decorate

A GREAT START TO THE DAY AND AN EASY BREAKFAST IF YOU'RE IN A HURRY. IF THE SMOOTHIE IS TOO THICK, ADD EXTRA SOY MILK, COW'S MILK, OR CHILLED WATER.

1 Whizz all the ingredients together in a food processor or blender until smooth.

2 Pour into tall glasses and serve dusted with a little ground cinnamon, and the glasses decorated with whole strawberries. Add straws and serve immediately.

nutrition facts	
energy	190 cal
	800 kJ
protein	10 g
fat	4 g
of which saturated	1.5 g
carbohydrate	30 g
fiber	1 g
cholesterol	9 mg
sodium	80 mg

index